INTRODUCTION TO TAROT

"This book is an excellent introduction to the Tarot for those of us who want to study this ancient art but do not know where to embark. It *[Introduction to Tarot]* is written in such a way that it stimulates the imagination and gently opens the door to the world of archetypes and magic."

—Candis Cantin Packard, author and creator of *Herbal Tarot*

"Susan Levitt's readable book is a perfect introduction to reading Tarot cards."

—Brian Williams, author and creator of *Renaissance Tarot,* *Pomo Tarot,* and *Minchiate Tarot*

"Susan Levitt's charming book offers newcomers a gentle and creative introduction to the Tarot. Neither oversimplified nor overcomplicated, **Introduction to Tarot** contains good basic ideas presented in an accessible and attractive way."

—Cynthia Giles, author of *The Tarot: History, Mystery, and Lore* and *The Tarot: Methods, Mastery, and More*

"Susan Levitt presents an engaging work for beginners with Tarot. I particularly like the section on soul cards."

—Pamela Eakins, author and creator of *Tarot of the Spirit*

INTRODUCTION TO TAROT

by Susan Levitt

U.S. GAMES
SYSTEMS, INC

PUBLISHED BY U.S. GAMES SYSTEMS, INC.
STAMFORD, CT • USA

Third Edition

10 9 8 7 6

Printed in China

Published by
U.S. Games Systems, Inc.
179 Ludlow Street
Stamford, CT 06902 USA
www.usgamesinc.com

Jody Boginski, Designer
AnnMarie McLaughlin, Editor

"You're nothing but a pack of cards!"

—Alice in Wonderland

This book is for all my tarot students—past, present, and future.

ACKNOWLEDGMENTS

Dedicated to the memory of Brian Williams; tarot master, exquisite artist, and brilliant scholar. I will always treasure his kindness, his humor, his generosity—and how he magically bridged the world of tarot from Renaissance Italy to modern day San Francisco.

Many thanks to my sister Char Levitt, best friend Neeltje de Haan, mentor Emilio Cruz, advisor Chuck Gutro, Susan Utell Little Bird, Kathy Stephens Little Dog, and tarot ace Donna Gillespie.

Much love and blessings to tarot goddesses Rachel Pollack, Mary K. Greer, Vicki Noble, and Ffiona Morgan; tarot divas Thalassa, Patricia Croteau, and Miss Monika Auerback; and my tarot family Stevee Postman, Stuart Kaplan, Gary Ross, James Wanless, Kevin Grey Harris, Candis Cantin Packard, Cynthia Giles, Pamela Eakins, Barbara Rapp, Alexandra and Ken Genetti, Ruth Ann and Wald Amberstone, Ed Buryn, Julia Cuccia-Watts, Kelesyn Winter, and Jim Schutte.

TABLE OF CONTENTS

PREFACE

I WAS 17 YEARS OLD IN 1972 when I first sought answers from the tarot. I inquired about working as a florist to support myself while I studied painting at The School of the Art Institute of Chicago. The final outcome card was the 8 of Cups. It showed a dissatisfied person walking away, wearing a heavy cloak.

Because I had already paid a deposit for classes, I ignored the tarot's prognosis and attended a floral arts school for the summer, received certification, and got a job at a hotel that autumn.

My experience working as a florist did not fulfill my expectation of working with the beauty of nature. All bouquets were copied from a floral delivery book.

Creativity and sculpture with flowers (or Japanese *ikibana)* was discouraged. After handling hundreds of roses, I grew to watch for thorns instead of admiring the blossoms, which had no scent because they were hothouse buds.

Adding to my dissatisfaction was my irritable boss. When I tried to talk to him about his bitter disposition, he screamed at me for the last time and I quit. I left the hotel as the cold Chicago wind blew down the street. I headed to the subway station, and was putting up the collar of my heavy winter coat when it hit me— I was reenacting the exact picture on the 8 of Cups! I was actually living the tarot.

Because the reading came true,

I had to have my own tarot deck and learn to read the cards. I went to the only place I knew of that sold tarot cards in Chicago, the Occult Bookshop located on North State Street.

I entered the store, which can best be described as *witchy*. It was stocked from floor to ceiling with every imaginable occult item, from pure and healing to negative and creepy. There were astrology maps, candles, oils, brews and elixirs, costumes, capes, and what appeared to be stuffed and mounted animals. I asked to see the tarot decks, and the large Thoth deck intrigued me. Its shamanic imagery perfectly mirrored the energy of the Occult Bookstore. I purchased the Thoth deck and Aleister Crowley's *Book of Thoth*. I read the book cover to cover that night. I understood it because of my childhood interest in fairy tales, mythology, Egyptian archeology, and my hobby (bordering on obsession) foreign languages. I had attended Hebrew school as a child, studied Latin in high school, and was reading Ezra Pound's translations from the Chinese when I was a teen. But, for me, Crowley resonated more than Pound, for he used symbols in a practical manner. Although I enjoyed reading about tarot, I discovered that one could understand the meanings of the cards simply by looking at the pictures.

My newfound interest in tarot was not well received. I was told that tarot was "the work of the devil." People actually said to me "You will burn in hell!" and "Get thee behind me, Satan!" I felt like a pioneer keeping alive the ancient mysteries. I didn't mind the "you will burn in hell" curses because hell was the accuser's personal vision, not mine. But the unsolicited and unwelcome attempts to cast out my demons really did upset me.

In 1980, I moved to Tucson, Arizona to attend graduate school in art history. People were even more anti-tarot there than in Chicago. I finished my studies and then pulled tarot cards to determine a better place for me to live where my soul would be content. My choices were either New York

Ace of Cups

City or San Francisco. New York was the Wheel of Fortune. San Francisco was the Ace of Cups. Both are excellent cards. But I chose the Ace of Cups because I am a Pisces with a grand water trine in my birth chart (Sun in Pisces trine Jupiter and Uranus in Cancer trine Saturn in Scorpio). I realized that in New York I would make more money, but I followed my heart.

On New Year's Day 1983, I moved to San Francisco. The reaction to my interest in tarot cards was the opposite of what I experienced in Chicago and Tucson. Many people *asked* me to read tarot for them. In 1986, I resigned from my job as an artist and became a professional tarot card reader. (I've found it more fulfilling to read tarot than to paint.) Soon my clients asked me to teach them how to read tarot cards. I typed up a few notes and passed them out in my classes. Eventually the notes grew and ended up as this book.

Fortune

I invite you to join me and share the mystery.

THE SEVEN CHAKRAS

INTRODUCTION
Tarot *and* Chakras

O F THE MANY FORMS OF DIVINATION, tarot stands alone in its
artistry and clarity of information. By working with the universal
symbols of tarot, one is linked to the diversity of life experiences. When
simply holding a tarot deck, one is connected to the *anima mundi* (world
soul), the collective unconscious, the healing qualities of the human
heart, and psyche.

To fully comprehend tarot as a tool for spiritual healing, one needs to
become familiar with the ancient Hindu system of the seven *chakras*.
(*Chakra* means wheel in Sanskrit.) Each chakra represents different energy
patterns in our body. When all seven chakras are balanced, one can attain
their highest level of energy and creative potential.

The first chakra, located at the base of the spine, correlates to basic survival issues. In times of war or extreme illness, this chakra is strongly
activated. Once survival issues are resolved, procreation can occur
through the second chakra, the genital area, which channels sexual and
creative energy. The third chakra, located in the solar plexus, represents
power and the pursuit of material gain. Most people in the world, con-
sumed with the mundane challenges of everyday existence, are focused
on in these three lower chakras.

It is the fourth chakra, the heart center of love, caring, and compassion
that introduces the realm of transcendence and spirituality. The fourth

chakra is personified as the loving kindness of Buddha, the sacred heart of Jesus Christ, and in the merciful goodness of the Chinese goddess Quan Yin, among others. Religious and spiritual disciplines that emphasize living from the heart, (such as "Love thy neighbor as thyself") all reside within the fourth chakra.

Moving upwards from the heart, the fifth chakra is located in the throat. This chakra is associated with the spoken work and the power of words to heal (and harm). The sixth chakra, also referred to as the "third eye," is located between the eyebrows. It is associated with creative vision and clairvoyance. Inspiration comes through the seventh chakra, the crown center. In our modern technological environment, many of us have closed the seventh chakra to avoid being over-whelmed by external stimuli. But in a peaceful, meditative environment we can open the seventh chakra to receive spiritual guidance.

Working with the magic of tarot symbolism brings us to the heart center, above the mundane realities of the first three chakras. On a higher metaphysical level, working with tarot cards can open up the seventh chakra of divine inspiration and the sixth chakra of creative vision. Insight communicated through the fifth chakra, tempered with compassion of the fourth chakra, can create a tarot interpretation of the most effective healing alchemy.

Too often tarot cards are used to answer questions concerning lower chakra activities. For example, a question such as "Does my boyfriend still want me?" activates first chakra survival fears, second chakra sexual concerns, and third chakra power issues. The heart is not present.

But the same question asked as "What can I do to develop the best in our relationship?" can open one up to a sixth chakra creative vision. The statement, "I don't like my boss" can be addressed to the tarot as "How can the problems I experience with my boss help me to grow and become aware?"

Elevate your questions by raising them to the highest form possible. Interpret the cards with wisdom, compassion, creativity, intuition, and sensitivity. This is the path of powerful magic and transformation. Manifesting and expressing our highest essence is our birthright as human beings. We can use the tarot to heal, achieve goals, attain vision, and create peaceful solutions to the many problems that seem to overwhelm us.

This book is for everyone who wishes to use tarot as a tool for personal growth and transformation. More importantly, it is a plea for sane living by giving equal value to both feminine and masculine energies, both of which are well represented in the tarot deck. It is in this balance of light and dark that we can heal ourselves and then heal others.

CHAPTER 1

STRUCTURE OF TAROT
About Tarot Cards

TAROT CARDS were invented in Renaissance Italy in the early 15th century. They were originally a variation of playing cards with four suits. Tarot cards, the Italian *tarocchi,* were used primarily for playing card games, not for divination, study, or meditation. Tarot gained an occult usage in late 18th century France. The modern word *tarot* is of French origin and is pronounced "taro" with the final "t" silent.

Tarot was studied in England by the occult group The Golden Dawn during the end of the 19th century and into the beginning of the 20th century. In 1910, the Rider company of London published a tarot deck designed by Golden Dawn member Arthur Edward Waite and illustrated by Golden Dawn artist Pamela Colman Smith. The deck was very innovative because every card showed a picture that told a story. This deck is now called the Rider-Waite tarot deck.

Avant-garde occultist Aleister Crowley, also a member of the Golden Dawn, designed the Thoth tarot deck in 1944. Illustrated by Lady Freida Harris, the cards were unique because they

Arthur Edward Waite

Pamela Colman Smith

Aleister Crowley

included astrological symbols, Hebrew letters, and occult references. Thoth was the ancient Egyptian ibis-headed god of communication, medicine, and metaphysical wisdom. His Nubian name is Tehuti. His correlation in the ancient Greek pantheon is Hermes (Roman Mercury), the messenger god and guide of souls in the underworld. The alchemical god Hermes Trimegustus (thrice great Hermes) is a form of Thoth.

The Rider-Waite and the Aleister Crowley Thoth tarot decks illustrate this book.

Tarot cards illustrate symbols and myths that are allegorical of life experiences and situations. By reading your personal experience in the cards, you become part of the collective whole of human experience, what wise scholars refer to as the *akashic record,* the astral record of all that has ever been and ever will be in existence. By working with the oracle of tarot, one is no longer alone in an isolated struggle for clarity; you are part of a greater whole.

The Four Elements

THE GREATER WHOLE OF THE COSMOS is based on a structural foundation composed of the four elements: fire, water, air, and earth. These four elements are symbolized as the wand, cup, sword, and pentacle (disk) suits of the tarot cards. The four elements also correspond to four directions and colors: south (red), west (black), east (yellow), and north (white) respectively. These four colors represent the four races of humanity.

The four elements of fire, water, air, and earth are found in many other magical and spiritual systems such as the Native American medicine wheel, the four corners of pagan ritual, the four elements of astrology, and the four elements of the alchemi-

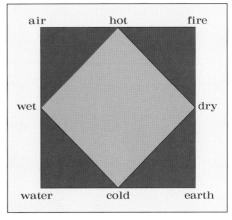

The four elements and their four qualities from ancient Egypt 5,000 B.C.*

cal schools of medieval Europe. Through alchemy one can change the base self into gold—radiant and rare. By combining the elements, we can transform reality.

The truth is one, the paths are many. There are other ways to create order out of chaos by combining elements. For example, the ancient Chinese Taoists understood the cosmos to be composed of five elements: Fire, earth, metal, water, and wood. The ancient East Indian Vedics interpreted the universe in three elements, or *doshas: vata* (air), *pitta* (fire), and *kapha* (water and earth). But four elements are the basis of tarot.

*James, George G.M. *Stolen Legacy*; Julian Richardson Assoc. Pub., 1954.

FIRE

In tarot, the exciting masculine element fire represents will, drive, destiny, action, adventure, creativity, and spirit in action. The symbol for fire is a wand, a blazing wand of power. In a regular playing deck, fire is represented by the suit of clubs. Fire is the phallus ejaculating seeds of creativity. A few fire myths and legends include the fire stealer Prometheus, Satan and his flames, the Phoenix that rises from its own ashes, and Apollo in his sun chariot. Fire Goddesses include lioness-headed Sekmet of ancient Egypt and sun goddess Ameratsu of Japan. In astrology, the fire signs are Sagittarius ♐, Aries♈, and Leo♌.

WATER

In tarot, the element water is the nurturing, feminine element that represents emotions, intuition, spiritual belief, reflection, joy, faith, and love. Water is symbolized as a cup or chalice. In a conventional playing deck, the suit of hearts represents water. Water is the essence of life, the sea of fertility, the amniotic fluid of the womb, and the womb of the Ocean Mother from whom emerged all life on earth. According to the ancient Taoists, water is the strongest element for it can flow around any obstacle in its path without changing essence. Water myths and legends include the search for the fountain of youth, the quest for the holy grail, Noah and the

FIRE

WATER

SEAL OF
SOLOMON

ark, Jonah in the belly of the whale, the waters of St. John the Baptist, mermaids and sirens, and Poseidon (Roman Neptune) the god of the ocean. In astrology, the water signs are Pisces ♓, Cancer ♋, and Scorpio ♏.

Together, the wands and cups suits of the tarot have an even grander symbolic significance. The mixture of fire and water creates an alchemical balance of emotion put into action, or action stemming from compassionate emotion. One defines the other and creates a balanced polarity of yang (masculine fire) and yin (feminine water); The harmonious blend of day and night, light and dark. For example, when we inhale, our lungs expand to the most yang point. When we exhale our lungs contract to the most yin point. This cycle continues, just as high noon progresses to midnight and returns to high noon. The interplay between masculine and feminine elements is the essence of life. Tarot imagery illustrates the balance of male and female, fire and water, light and dark, yin and yang. It is believed that death occurs when yin and yang separate.

In alchemical script, the symbol for fire is a triangle and the symbol for water is an inverted triangle. When superimposed one upon the other they create the six-pointed star of the *Kabbalah*, the Hebrew mysteries, known as the Seal of Solomon (Sulyman) or the Star of David. The six-pointed star is also an ancient Vedic tantric symbol of male and female union.

AIR

In tarot, the masculine element air represents the mind, mental activity, knowledge, intellect, thoughts, ideas, and communication. The symbol for air is a sword, which can cut through matter with clarity and swiftness. In a regular playing card deck, the suit of spades represents air. Air myths and legends include the Tower of Babel, the winged messenger god Mercury (Greek Hermes), and the smoke of the peace pipe. The power of communication is valued throughout history. In astrology, the air signs are Gemini ♊, Libra ♎, and Aquarius ♒.

EARTH

The fourth element is stable, feminine earth, which represents nature, the material world, money, career, physical health, tangible goods, and the concrete reality of our Mother Earth who we walk on every day. The symbol for earth is a pentacle or a disk. Medieval European tarot decks depicted the element earth as golden coins. In a regular playing card deck, earth is the suit of diamonds. Because we are in a physical body, earth-plane reality is a constant awareness. Earth myths and legends include the Minotaur of Crete, the golden calf, Atlas carrying the world on his shoulders, Persephone in the underworld, and the goose that laid the golden egg. In astrology, the earth signs are Virgo ♍, Capricorn ♑, and Taurus ♉.

Together, air and earth create a male and female polarity, just as fire and water are polarized. The mixture of air and earth is the alchemical balance of making ideas reality and changing physical reality through thoughts and ideas. The legend of the sword in the stone is an archetypal example of mind overcoming matter. A new development in Western medicine is to focus on the link between health (earth) and attitude (air).

The Minor Arcana *and* The Court Cards

THE FOUR SUITS OF THE TAROT DECK ARE Wands, Cups, Swords, and Pentacles/Disks. There are ten cards for each suit numbered one (ace) through ten. These forty cards are referred to as the Minor Arcana. Arcana is derived from the word arcane, meaning hidden or secret.

THE NUMBERS ONE THROUGH TEN HAVE SYMBOLIC MEANING:

1 One (Ace) is the number of new beginnings and opportunities.
2 Two is a number of partnership and balance.
3 Three is a number of trinity and magic.
4 Four is a number of foundation and completion.
5 Five is a number of strife and chaos.
6 Six is a number of perfection and beauty.
7 Seven is a number of spiritual seeking and questing.
8 Eight is a number of both infinity and stability.
9 Nine is a master number of magic and is the highest single digit number.
10 Ten is the top number of fulfillment and harvest.

In the tarot deck there are also 16 court cards, or royal figures. They represent the *anima* and *animus*, the female and male attributes of the elements. The court cards also represent stages of maturity. Depending on the suit and level of maturity, a court card represents a combination of element and personality. The King or Prince represents mastery, power, and strength. The Queen embodies her element with depth and maturity. Knights denote action, quest, and movement. Pages represent exploration, seeking, and learning. (Court card personalities are discussed in detail in later chapters.)

The remaining twenty-two cards of the tarot deck are referred to as the Major Arcana, which are discussed in the next chapter. These are the trump cards that tell the story of the journey of the individual soul. They are richly symbolic pictures of a very old mystery.

Turn the page and begin the journey...

CHAPTER 2:

THE MAJOR ARCANA
The Fool's Journey

THE JOURNEY THROUGH THE 22 MAJOR ARCANA CARDS is a passage through the archetypal experiences of humanity and the many states of being, as from our collective unconscious. The number 22 is significant because in numerology 22 is one of the master numbers (as are 11 and 33). Twenty-two is the number of the master builder, and the journey through the 22 Major Arcana cards is masterfully built on a structure of cycles. Tarot archetypes are as fresh today as they were in medieval Spain, mythic Atlantis, or ancient Egypt, for universal life experiences transcend boundaries of space and time.

0 · FOOL

OUR TAROT JOURNEY BEGINS with the first Major Arcana card: The freedom-loving FOOL. He represents new beginnings as he starts his heroic quest for self knowledge. In his naïve innocence, the FOOL is very creative for he does not yet know rules or limitations. He is the court jester, village idiot, clown, time traveler, speaker of truth, prodigal son, and the hero with 1,000 faces. His number is 0, the empty vessel waiting to be filled. He is ruled by the planet Uranus ♅, the planet of revolution and liberation. The FOOL brings exciting energy to break you from boredom or stagnation.

This card brings a sense of casting all cares to the wind. Logic, planning, and order are not involved. Instead, magical synchronicities and lucky serendipitous events can occur. To be open, free, and spontaneous may be FOOLish behavior. But as his journey progresses, such FOOLishness does lead to mastery and wisdom.

The Rider-Waite deck shows a youth about to step off a cliff. He could crash downward, or instead soar to the highest heavens because he took a creative risk and has faith. The Crowley deck shows the FOOL with all things there for the taking. The Hebrew letter at the bottom of the card is *aleph*, meaning ox.

DIVINATORY MEANING:
Now is the time to take a risk or seek adventure because you are guided by faith, folly, or fancy. Be open to new opportunities. Those who are uncomfortable with change may dislike experiencing the FOOL card because they are not used to freedom and taking creative risks with an unknown outcome.

1 · MAGICIAN *and* MAGUS

Once the FOOL takes a risk, he finds his power in the next card, the mighty MAGICIAN. Under the MAGICIAN'S influence, all endeavors that require willpower are manifested. This is a powerful man who can work magic and heal.

In the Rider-Waite deck, the MAGICIAN holds a wand in his upraised hand. The wand conducts energy from heaven to earth. On the MAGI-CIAN'S table are symbols of the four elements: the wand of fire △, the cup of water ▽, the sword of air △, and the pentacle of earth ▽. All four magical tools can be used as needed. The MAGICIAN is called the MAGUS in the Crowley deck. The plural form of the word magus is *magi*. The three wise men, or magi (magicians), visited the Christ child at his humble birth in a manger. They brought the gifts of frankincense which is sacred to the sun, myrrh which is sacred to the moon, and gold which is the alchemist's metal. The Crowley deck MAGUS is depicted having a breakthrough of power and perception. The wings on his feet and the caduceus on his head are symbols of Mercury ☿ (Greek Hermes), the messenger who connects humanity with the divine. The Hebrew letter on the bottom of the MAGUS card is *beth*, meaning house.

DIVINATORY MEANING:
You are completely powerful and can manifest your goals. You are experiencing magical strength and can actualize your desires through your own creativity and will.

2 · PRIESTESS

The MAGICIAN cannot be fully realized without his *anima* (female half), the mystic PRIESTESS. While the MAGICIAN has physical magical tools, the PRIESTESS possesses inner magical tools. She is ruled by the Moon ☽ and represents the eternal feminine. She is the psychic healer who knows the great women's mysteries of birth, life, and death. She embodies wisdom, serene knowledge, intuitive judgment, and common sense.

In the Rider-Waite deck, the PRIESTESS is enthroned with the moon and water at her feet. The moon and water are feminine symbols of the ever-changing lunar cycles linked to tides and menstrual flow. She wears the crown of the goddesses Isis and Hathor. The PRIESTESS sits harmoniously between two strong pillars. The black pillar symbolizes the receptive principle. Black is the color of night and the womb, the deep mystery far within. The white pillar represents the active principle of expansion, light, and activity. Behind the PRIESTESS is a garden of pomegranates and palms, symbolic of female and male genitalia. In her lap is a scroll which reads *tora*, which are the first five books of Moses, the Old Testament of

Genesis, Exodus, Leviticus, Numbers, and Deuteronomy. Tora is an anagram for *taro* (the cards) and *rota*, the ever-revolving wheel. The Crowley Thoth deck PRIESTESS is veiled, and she weaves light energy that is magnified by crystals. She has the huntress' bow of the goddess Artemis (Roman Diana). Crystals are at her feet, as is the self-sustained camel who carries within the nurturing waters. The Hebrew letter on the bottom of the PRIESTESS card is *gimel*, meaning camel.

DIVINATORY MEANING:
This card indicates strong destiny—your affairs are safely in the lap of the Goddess. You are empowered to open yourself to your feminine receptive nature. Record your dreams and flow with the sensitivity and wisdom of your intuition. This is an opportunity to listen to and trust your inner voice. You are safe.

3·EMPRESS

Next on our journey from the exhaulted PRIESTESS is the EMPRESS enthroned. She represents the full cornucopia of an abundant harvest. She is the nurturing Earth Mother, the physical manifestation of the inner spirit of the PRIESTESS. The EMPRESS is full of life, and symbolizes the fertile womb. Birth, the amazing act of creation, is in her realm. Both the EMPRESS and PRIESTESS are seated on thrones. The EMPRESS is ruled by the planet Venus ♀, the goddess of love and beauty (Greek Aphrodite).

The EMPRESS represents the harvest of all that has been planted. The creative energy of the EMPRESS satisfies the FOOL'S venturing, as the balance of the MAGICIAN'S masculine energy and the PRIESTESS' feminine energy combine to create the child/harvest of the EMPRESS.

In the Rider-Waite image, the crowned EMPRESS sits before a background of lush vegetation and a gently curving river. The Venus symbol ♀ decorates her heart-shaped shield. In the Crowley deck, the enthroned EMPRESS is shown with the fertility symbols of the crescent moon and a swan with cygnets. The Hebrew letter on the bottom of the EMPRESS card is *daleth*, meaning door.

DIVINATORY MEANING:
Your energies are balanced and harmonious. You will be fortunate and secure with material matters such as finding a suitable job or a place to live. The EMPRESS is ruled by Venus, so adorn yourself with jewelry and your finest clothing.

4 · EMPEROR

Thus far all seems blessed on the journey through the archetypes, but then the fiery EMPEROR appears to command the garden. He represents power and domination. The EMPEROR is a pioneer, leader, and explorer. He is a warrior who has the strength to go forth and succeed, a man of action. In imperial China, the EMPEROR'S symbol was the Dragon that represented masculine yang energy. (The EMPRESS' symbol was the Phoenix that represented female yin energy.) EMPERORS throughout history, from Caesar to Napoleon, possess the traits of absolute power, dogmatic authority, and iron will; which if not properly handled can lead to corruption. When successfully channeled, the EMPEROR can be a dynamic, strong, focused, and incisive catalyst for change and creation. Yet he often wants things his way only. He can be intolerant, even ruthless, if others do not agree with his methods. Or he may quickly lose interest and not complete what was originally initiated in an enthusiastic way.

Because the EMPEROR is ruled by the astrology sign Aries ♈, rams surround his throne in both the Rider-Waite and Crowley Thoth decks. The EMPEROR is portrayed holding the scepter of masculine energy in his right hand and the orb of feminine energy in his left hand. Therefore he possesses the power of balanced action. In the Rider-Waite image, the river of life runs behind the EMPEROR'S throne signifying masculinity, power, and strength. In the Crowley deck, the EMPEROR looks to his right. (You may note that if you lay the EMPEROR and the EMPRESS cards down side by side, they are looking at each other.) The Hebrew letter on the bottom of the card is *tzddi*, meaning fishhook.

DIVINATORY MEANING:
There is potential for much growth and movement, and the ability to start projects with fiery passion, leadership, power, and enthusiasm. Goals must be aggressively pursued. This is not a time for passive inactivity. Be aware to not inflict your will on others. Resist the urge to tell them what to do, even if you believe it is for their own good.

5·HIEROPHANT

The EMPEROR has conquered and is trying to establish control. However, he is too impatient to rule in an organized manner. Hence the stern HIEROPHANT appears to create laws to maintain peace and order. He establishes his hierarchy. His authoritative rulership can be one-dimensional, patriarchal, and repressive. When the HIEROPHANT appears, there will be structure and order in the land, such as rigid societal rules that dictate one must work from nine to five, and that children must attend school from nine to three. The HIEROPHANT'S system cannot be changed, for it is ruled by Taurus ♉, a fixed earth sign. The HIEROPHANT'S positive attribute is that he can be a teacher, father figure, or spiritual authority on religious issues. He can enforce codes of conduct that offer structure and security. His word is law. This card often appears when one must become a part of an organized structure or ritual (such as a school curriculum, military service, or the corporate world).

HIEROPHANT is derived from the word hierarchy, which means a government by priests and other clergy. This adds further insight to the meaning of this card.

The Rider-Waite deck shows a religious figure, an enthroned Pope seated between two gray columns, with two priests below him.

The Crowley deck shows the HIEROPHANT figure surrounded by the four elements' signs in the four corners of the card. The lion represents Leo ♌, fixed fire. The eagle represents Scorpio ♏, fixed water. The human head represents Aquarius ♒, fixed air. In the left corner, the fixed earth, Taurus bull ♉ is shown again. The Hebrew letter at the bottom of the card is *vav*, meaning nail.

DIVINATORY MEANING:
Accept your niche within his structure, conform, learn from the discipline, and plan it to your advantage. If the rigidity is too unbearable, you may choose to rebel and leave. In rare instances, this card may indicate a stern yet loving patriarch whose word is law.

6 · LOVERS

The next archetype on the tarot journey is the blissful LOVERS. This card balances and unites the extremes of the freedom-loving energies of the first four cards (FOOL, MAGICIAN, PRIESTESS, and EMPRESS) and the dominating energies of the last two cards (EMPEROR and HIEROPHANT). The LOVERS is a blending of male and female and is ruled by the androgynous astrology sign of Gemini, the twins ♊. This tarot card illustrates the sacred marriage of dark and light within one's own being; synthesis of the

subjective and knowing inner self and the outer and active observing self. Part of the LOVER'S mystery is the exhilaration and passion of falling in love. On a spiritual level, this card represents the marriage of duality.

Both decks show a couple joined in happy union. In the Rider-Waite deck, the nude female figure, like Eve in the Garden of Eden, stands beside a fruited tree which is encoiled by the wise serpent. The nude male stands beside a flaming tree of life and passion. Instead of being separated as in the biblical tale, this couple is united. Their union is blessed by an angel. In the Crowley deck, the couple is blessed by a god-like figure. This deck also indicates light and dark adults and children, and the red lion and white eagle of alchemy. Blindfolded Cupid (Greek Eros), the son of Venus, is posed to shoot his arrow of love. The Hebrew letter on the bottom of the LOVERS card is *zain*, meaning sword.

DIVINATORY MEANING:
More than the concept of finding a Lover, this card is also the alchemical blend within yourself. The point at which you feel in love with the world, and more importantly, in love with yourself. A positive mental outlook and strong self-esteem leaves one open to experience healthy, loving relationships. Also indicated is the ability to freely express emotions and to trust your feelings. This is a very fortunate card.

7·CHARIOT

After the balancing of the previous LOVERS card, the focused CHARIOT emerges to act independently. The CHARIOTEER is drawn forward on a strong solid path. He travels through life with a sense of purpose, discipline, and direction. The CHARIOT'S armor is not to keep people out, but is instead a protective shield. Ancient Mediterranean images of CHARIOTEERS show strong youths enjoying their games and races. The Greek goddess Athena (Roman Minerva) is often depicted in her CHARIOT.

Roman heroes rode chari-
ots in triumphant proces-
sions. This card is ruled by
the astrology sign Cancer
♋, which denotes cardi-
nal (moving) water.

In the Rider-Waite deck,
the CHARIOT is pulled by
two sphinxes, one light
and one dark. The crowned
CHARIOTEER wears a gar-
ment of lunar crescents
on his shoulders and mag-
ical symbols on his skirt.
He holds a large wand
indicating mastery. In the Crowley Thoth deck, the CHAR-
IOT is pulled by four sphinxes representing the four
elements; therefore the path is balanced. The crab on the
Crowley CHARIOTEER'S crown symbolizes the astrology
sign Cancer ♋. The Hebrew letter on the bottom of the
CHARIOT is *cheth,* meaning fence.

DIVINATORY MEANING:
*Your path is clear and focused. Energies are harnessed, progress is
made, and goals can be attained. You are a triumphant, victorious, and
successful winner. You can cover much ground.*

8 · STRENGTH *or* 11 · LUST

The next card in the Rider-Waite deck is radiant STRENGTH. After the victories of the CHARIOT, one can experience their magical STRENGTH. This card is ruled by the astrology sign Leo ♌. It shows a woman with her arm around a lion. The lion is her animal totem (or "familiar"), because the animal's spirit and essence are shared with the woman. She embodies masterful leonine qualities while retaining her human intelligence. Although lions are often associated with men (i.e. Hercules and the lion)

in this archetype a woman is with the lion, which further indicates a gentle well-balanced STRENGTH.

The Crowley deck calls this card LUST, or lust for life. For the mundane sex-focused person, the card represents sexual LUST. For others, LUST denotes Leo creativity with the symbols of sperm and ovum on the top of the card. The sperm is depicted swimming to fertilize the ovum. A powerfully passionate and fiery woman rides a lion creature. The Hebrew letter on bottom of the card is *teth*, meaning serpent.

DIVINATORY MEANING:
You will be strong and powerful in your endeavors. You can be in control of the situation and face difficulties head on. You possess courage, fortitude, and abundant STRENGTH.

Note that the 11 LUST card and the 8 ADJUSTMENT card differ from the card order of the Rider-Waite deck. Crowley changed the order of these two Major Arcana cards in the eighth and eleventh positions because he felt that then the 22 Major Arcana cards corresponded to the 22 letters of the Hebrew alphabet (or aleph–beth, the letters on the 0 Fool and 1 Magician).

9 · HERMIT

Now that the soul has healed in the LOVERS, it has moved onto a path of clarity with the CHARIOT, and is powerful with STRENGTH (or balanced with ADJUSTMENT. See page 50.) It is now time to reflect on previous actions. This brings us to the contemplative HERMIT. The HERMIT marks an important place on the FOOL'S journey. Number nine is the last of the cardinal numbers and for the first time it is appropriate to completely stop and contemplate what has been learned and experienced so far. The HERMIT carries his own lantern, light of illumination. The answers are within us, if one is willing to be alone and quietly meditate. There are myriad spiritual traditions of the Hermit: Taoists in the remote mountains of China; medieval European HER-MITS' mystical realization of God; East Indian yogis, masters, and saints; the lone vision quests of Native Americans; and the walk-abouts of the Australian aborigines. All are solitary experiences that bring one closer to self knowledge and enlightenment. Due to his contemplative nature, the HERMIT is ruled by self-analyzing Virgo ♍.

In the Rider-Waite deck, the HERMIT holds a lantern that encases a six-pointed star. Light shines to illuminate the path. In the Crowley deck, the HERMIT is surrounded by grains of the fertile earth. A sperm shoots upward, the male seed. A snake wrapped around an egg symbolizes the fertility and creativity of the HERMIT'S vision.

At his feet is Cerberus, the three-headed dog that guards the Underworld and the Mysteries of the Dead. The Hebrew letter on the bottom of the HERMIT card is *yod*, which is the first letter of the name of God, Yehovah. This symbolizes the archetype of the wise father.

DIVINATORY MEANING:
A time to look within and be alone. This is not a social time, but instead a period of silent reflection and solitary quest for inner vision. This card is easy to accept for the introvert who enjoys solitude, meditation, and quiet walks. But it may represent a challenge for an extrovert who enjoys attention, activity, or interaction with many companions. To accept the HERMIT'S way leads to wisdom.

10 · WHEEL OF FORTUNE

The wise HERMIT leaves his solitude to venture into the world. All is superb with this excellent card: the lucky WHEEL OF FORTUNE. The WHEEL in the sky has turned and all is magically blessed and serendipitous. Opportunity abounds. WHEEL OF FORTUNE is ruled by the bountiful god Jupiter ♃ (Greek Zeus). Jupiter is the largest planet. The expansive energy of this card is like Santa Claus bringing a big bag of gifts and goodies. The WHEEL is a universal symbol of healing, change, and transformation. In Buddhism, it is denoted by the WHEEL of *samsara*, the endless cycles of reincarnation. In Native American cultures, it is represented by the Medicine WHEEL, the sacred hoop.

The iconography of the Rider-Waite deck depicts the WHEEL OF FORTUNE with the word *taro*, the same anagram of *tora* and *rota* as seen on the PRIESTESS card. More anagrams are *ator*, Latin for speak, and *ator* (Hathor), an ancient Egyptian mother goddess depicted as a cow. In the biblical tale, Moses threw down the Ten Commandments because the Israelites were worshipping a "golden calf." This golden calf was Hathor. The occultists of the Golden Dawn interpreted *rota taro tora ator* to mean the WHEEL of tarot speaks the laws of Hathor. The Hebrew letters on the WHEEL OF FORTUNE, read counter-clockwise, are *yod, heh, vav,* and *heh*. These four letters are considered the name of God, often pronounced in English as "Jehovah." *Yod* symbolizes fire, *heh* water, *vav* air, and *heh* earth—the four elements. The sphinx on the card symbolizes the balance of the four elements. The snake represents change through the shedding of skin. The Egyptian jackal-headed god Anubis, Lord of Becoming, represents transformation. The four fixed elements are shown in the four corners: Aquarius-air, Scorpio-water, Leo-fire, and Taurus-earth. The Crowley deck depicts the WHEEL and the sphinx, Hermanubis (Hermes and Anubis), and Typhon, the Greek name for the Egyptian god Set. One of Typhon's roles was god of the deserts. (From his hot breath is derived the word "typhoon.") The Hebrew letter on the bottom of the card is *kalph*, meaning palm of the hand.

DIVINATORY MEANING:
Doors will open and all things will be much better than you can possibly imagine. Prosperity will descend on you. You will evolve out of a situation that is getting you nowhere. Set your sights high, and Jupiter will set them even higher and deliver.

11 · JUSTICE *and* 8 · ADJUSTMENT

FORTUNE manifested with the turn of the WHEEL. It is followed by honest JUSTICE which represents mental balance and harmonious action. This archetype is based on the laws of nature as well as human ethics. JUS-TICE is associated with the Greek goddess Themis, holder of the scales of truth. Themis and the earth goddess Gaia were sacred at the famous oracle of Delphi in ancient Greece. Qualities of JUSTICE were also associated with the Babylonian goddess Tiamat, who bestowed benevolent laws upon the first kings. The ancient Egyptian goddess Ma'at, who predates Greek culture by millenniums, held the original scales of truth. She balanced the heart of the deceased against the weight of her ostrich feather to determine a heart light with spirit or heavy with hatred. In Egyptian hieroglyphs, her feather means the word "truth." Worldwide, the concept of JUSTICE determines laws, establishes codes of conduct, guides social behavior, and helps to resolve disputes.

The Rider-Waite deck depicts a crowned woman upon a throne holding an upraised sword, symbol of air, and a set of balanced scales. Crowley calls this card ADJUSTMENT and it has the same meaning as JUSTICE. The sword held by the central figure symbol-izes a balanced mind. Within her scales are the symbols Alpha and Omega, the first and last letters of the Greek alphabet; Opportunity to initiate a new begin-ning which leads to a fulfilled completion. JUSTICE and ADJUST-MENT are ruled by the element air and the astrology sign Libra ♎. Therefore there is also an indica-tion that a relationship is worth developing to learn balance in partnership. The Hebrew letter on the bottom of the ADJUSTMENT card is *lamed*, meaning cattle prod.

DIVINATORY MEANING:
Balance body, mind, emotions, and spirit. Create an honest solution to all situations in order to restore harmony and fairness. The best solution may require generous compromise by both parties. Due to the Libran influence, this card can also indicate partnership.

12 · HANGED MAN

The WHEEL has turned and all is balanced with JUSTICE (or vitalized with LUST in the Crowley Thoth deck). But the FOOL'S journey has nowhere to go next. All avenues are exhausted. Hence we arrive at the lone HANGED MAN, an image of a man stuck, suspended upside down, with a halo of light around his head. He is on a similar, but higher plane than the HERMIT, for the HANGED MAN is related to spiritual awareness, surrender, and release. Ruled by Neptune Ψ (Greek Poseidon) god of the ocean, the HANGED MAN grapples with illusions and upsets. \

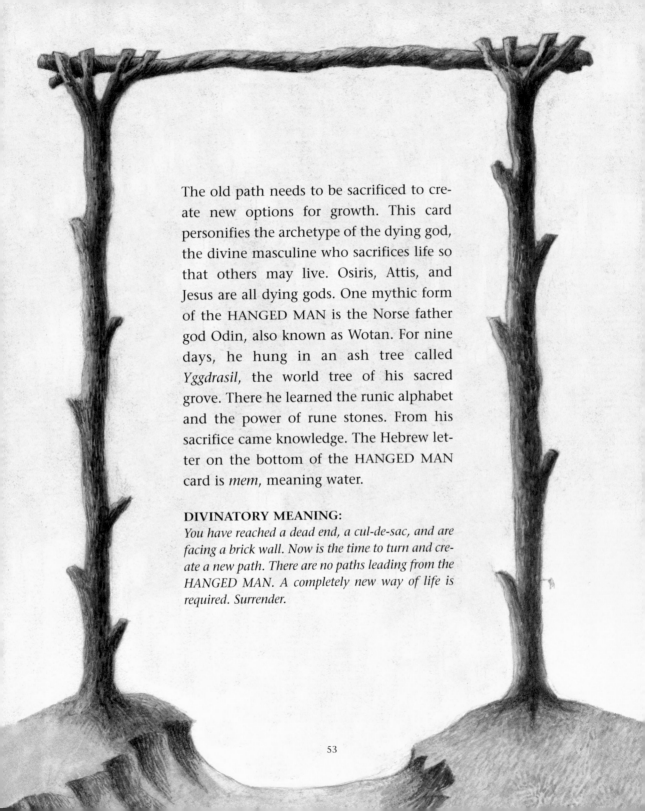

The old path needs to be sacrificed to create new options for growth. This card personifies the archetype of the dying god, the divine masculine who sacrifices life so that others may live. Osiris, Attis, and Jesus are all dying gods. One mythic form of the HANGED MAN is the Norse father god Odin, also known as Wotan. For nine days, he hung in an ash tree called *Yggdrasil*, the world tree of his sacred grove. There he learned the runic alphabet and the power of rune stones. From his sacrifice came knowledge. The Hebrew letter on the bottom of the HANGED MAN card is *mem*, meaning water.

DIVINATORY MEANING:
You have reached a dead end, a cul-de-sac, and are facing a brick wall. Now is the time to turn and create a new path. There are no paths leading from the HANGED MAN. A completely new way of life is required. Surrender.

13 · DEATH

Once one is able to accept the HANGED MAN, DEATH will enter and kill the old path. In this way, a rebirth to a new experience will manifest. Although the DEATH card is often feared, it is actually an unbelievably powerful and positive card of transformation, because DEATH precedes rebirth. One must clear away the old to make way for the new. Although the DEATH card may be difficult to experience, it is cathartic. Life is a series of deaths and rebirths, and the DEATH card cleanses and heals.

In the Rider-Waite deck, DEATH is shown wearing black armor and arriving on horseback amid the plague. He holds a flag decorated with a white rose, a symbol of purity. Three human figures before him respond in different ways. A priest is protected by his faith, a youth looks away, and an innocent child offers a bouquet of flowers. But all three will eventually die, which is the fate of all who are born. Yet in the background of the card is a sunrise to herald the dawn of a new day.

The Crowley deck shows DEATH as the grim reaper itself. Behind it are the souls yet to be reincarnated and experiences yet to be enacted. DEATH is ruled by the deep waters of Scorpio ♏. The symbol of Scorpio is the scorpion, a creature which can harm. The card also depicts the Scorpio snake that sheds its skin to emerge as a new snake. On the crown of the DEATH figure is a phoenix. This mythological bird flew so close to the sun that it burned—then rose anew from its own ashes. The phoenix myth represents the highest form of rebirth and renewal. The Hebrew letter on the bottom of the card is *nun*, which means fish.

There are myriad forms of DEATH, but two major ones emerge. One way to approach DEATH is to resist and go screaming and clawing all the way, feeling as if your whole world has collapsed. The other way to experience the DEATH card is to anticipate it, and then you can open yourself to accept it and understand it. One may even greet it, and work together to close the door behind you forever and embrace the new light.

DIVINATORY MEANING:
Accept the painful realization that things cannot continue in the same manner. You will not die, but the situation will die. Find solace in the fact that DEATH precedes rebirth, and know that life itself is a series of deaths and rebirths.

14 · TEMPERANCE *and* 14 · ART

There is a lovely rebirth to be had with the next card, poetic TEMPER-ANCE. The word TEMPERANCE stems from the Latin *temperare*, to mix or blend. This is the way of the alchemist, not the puritanical temperance of abstinence. The Rider-Waite deck shows an angel mixing waters from two cups. This angel stands with one foot in the waters of the unconscious and one foot on solid earth; inspired yet grounded. On the angel's garment is an upward-pointed triangle, a symbol for fire, on a square, a symbol of earth. Above the square are the Hebrew letters *yod, heh, vav,* and *heh*, the name of God. Also illustrated are irises of springtime and a sunrise at the end of a pathway.

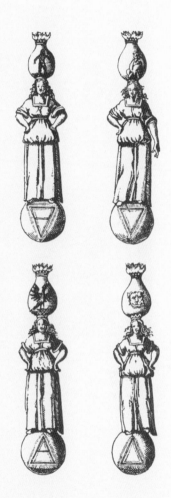

The Crowley deck calls this card ART. The transformed self changes base metal into gold by combining the masculine and feminine as the light and dark figures are blended into one. The light figure's hand pours water into the cauldron of renewal while the dark hand mixes fire into the brew. The red lion of summer on the LOVERS card has become white, and the white sulfur eagle has become red. Due to this iconographic transmutation, TEMPERANCE can be considered a higher form of the LOVERS card. On the cauldron is a raven and skull, pondering mortality. The crescent moons of a new beginning are overhead. There is an inscription referring to lapis, the alchemist's stone, in the interior of the earth. The Hebrew letter on the bottom of the ART card is *samekh*, meaning prop.

DIVINATORY MEANING:
A time of ARTistic creativity and beautiful inner realization. Events flow easily and smoothly and magic is in the air. It is easy to fulfill one's destiny and create positive change, and to integrate new experiences. Harmony and successful unions will arise.

15 · DEVIL

The next card, the sinister DEVIL, shows ignorance and confusion that needs to be dispersed. Be aware of deceit. Something is amiss and requires closer scrutiny. Examine the current situation and focus on clearing away any puzzlement. Just as the DEVIL can take many forms, the confusion of this card can manifest in a variety of ways. Often this card surfaces in an adulterous relationship. The DEVIL could also indicate poor communications or lack of honesty such as stealing and lying. The DEVIL is ruled by the horned Capricorn goat, who is depicted in both decks. Capricorn ♑ is an earth sign, so DEVIL conflicts often focus on greed and a desire for material goods.

In the Rider-Waite deck, a nude and horned couple are loosely chained. They are similar to the couple depicted in the LOVERS card. But on the DEVIL card, what began as a romance became enslavement. The Crowley Thoth deck shows a goat-like DEVIL figure and humans enclosed in two eggs. Four humans are male and four are female.

Prior to the advent of the Judeo-Christian-Islamic religions, the prototype of the DEVIL was often portrayed as a horned god, the playful wild man of the woods. In ancient Greece he was Dionysus (Roman Pan), the lover of the Goddess. But the tarot meaning is not based on playful, amusing, and erotic interpretations. Instead, this card is ruled by Saturn ♄, the planet of Capricorn; intrinsically, there is a quality of being restricted, limited, and blocked. The Hebrew letter on the bottom of the DEVIL card is *ayin*, meaning eye, in this case the evil eye.

DIVINATORY MEANING:
Materialism, overly concerned with money and success, dishonesty, illusion, and obsession. Allow some time for resolution of your situation and for confusion to disperse. Something is wrong that needs to be corrected. Now is not the time to act. The primitive god Saturn as Cronus, old father time, may unfold the answer, but all in good time.

16 · TOWER

If dispersal of confusion is slow in coming, do not fret. The lightning-struck TOWER will break you out of the prison created by the DEVIL. The TOWER arrives very suddenly and leaves just as quickly—it seems to come out of nowhere. DEATH and the HANGED MAN may linger, but the TOWER acts swiftly. Like DEATH, the TOWER is needed to destroy the restrictive structure that no longer serves your best interests for growth. This may be very upsetting to experience, but the result is total liberation. It is truly like breaking out of a prison. Ruled by Mars ♂ (Greek Ares), the god of war and courage, the TOWER often expresses itself as an upheaval. It is a battle quickly fought and quickly won—or lost.

The Rider-Waite deck shows two stricken figures falling from a blazing stone TOWER. Its golden domed roof is blasted away, struck by a bolt of lightening. The bits of falling fire are shaped like the Hebrew letter *yod*. The Crowley Thoth deck illustrates a TOWER felled by a great belch of fire as the eye of Shiva, the holy destroyer, stares above. The divine Vedic trinity of ancient India was composed of Brahma the creator, Vishnu the preserver, and Shiva the destroyer. Destruction serves a purpose to clear out old patterns to make way for new development. The Hebrew letter on the bottom of the TOWER card is *peh*, meaning mouth.

I cannot count how many times I have seen the TOWER card indicate divorce. But if you must conclude that the TOWER is always a catastrophic card, here is an amusing TOWER tale: A friend planned to sell her old car on a roadside, where people just parked their cars on weekends and bargained for the best deals. She pulled the TOWER card for the outcome of the car sale. At first there was concern about an accident, such as someone sideswiping her parked car. But her car sold that morning. Both buyer and seller were content. It was the immediacy of the sale that was manifested in the TOWER.

DIVINATORY MEANING:
Explosive liberation from the ivory tower that you set up to remain safe. Release of control. Sudden change of behavior. Don't bother to resist because change will happen so rapidly that you will immediately find a whole new world. There will be a new cast of characters in your life. This card can indicate divorce, moving to a new area, or a new job where everything is different.

17 · STAR

After being thrown from the TOWER into the dark of the night, the beautiful STAR appears and illuminates the new world. And what a lovely, peaceful world it is. The STAR card is a feminine card of understanding. There is a feeling of being connected with the entire universe. You are not a cog in a wheel—you *are* the cog, you *are* the wheel. Ruled by Aquarius ♒, the humanitarian water bearer of the zodiac, the STAR knows that all of humanity is a reflection of oneself. With the STAR as a focus, all the wisdom of the cosmos filters down. To receive the STAR is to be connected, and to possess faith, hope, and inspiration. On a mundane level, the STAR could mean receiving positive attention from others and feeling confident and talented, hence a STAR. But we are all STARS, and this card shows the deep connection among us all.

In both decks, a voluptuous female figure is shown beneath a beautiful STAR. She is radiant as she pours cool, healing crystalline waters. Water is a magical elixir in many spiritual traditions. This liquid is the water of the Holy Grail, the ambrosia of the Greek gods and goddesses, and the *amrit* (sweet nectar) of the Hindus. In the Rider-Waite deck, above the STAR maiden are eight eight-pointed stars. Seventeen reduces to 8 by adding 1 + 7. Like the TEMPERANCE card, the woman has one foot in water (spirit) and one on land (reality) as she pours from two full vases. The Crowley Thoth deck's STAR woman pours her waters beneath a seven-pointed star that spirals out light energy. Flowers and butterflies surround her, as does a glowing planet earth. The Hebrew letter on the bottom of the Crowley deck is *heh*, meaning window.

DIVINATORY MEANING:
Inspiration, vitality, hope, transformation, and regeneration. You have found your life's path and life's work. Step forward and be radiant. Do not hide your light. The STAR is also a card of healing, good health, calm, peace, harmony, and happiness.

18 · MOON

The next card, the ever-changing MOON, is up in the night sky with the STAR. All that flows is balanced in rhythm with the MOON. The MOON governs water on earth, ocean tides, women's reproductive cycles, the weather, and the fluids of the human body, animals, and plants. The MOON also rules emotions. The MOON card represents personal development, growth, change, and evolution. Just as the MOON in the night sky changes in phases, your MOON metamorphosis also occurs in phases. Your personality evolves as forgotten talents and interests surface.

There are eight lunar
phases each lunar month.
The eight phases can be understood
by observing plant growth. As above, so below.

1. The new MOON is like a seed planted in the earth, ready to grow, full
   of potential and energy for the journey. A new concept has taken hold.
   The new MOON rises at sunrise and sets at sunset. She is not visible in
   the sky.
2. The crescent MOON is the sprout. The seed has broken through the
   moist dark earth and reaches upward. One must break from the past,
   from the dark, moist, and familiar earth to venture forward. The crescent MOON rises midmorning and sets after sunset. She is the first
   visible sliver of MOON seen in the western sky in late afternoon and
   early evening.
3. The first quarter MOON is the growth phase. Roots venture deeper, the
   stem shoots up, and leaves form to create a new strong body. There is
   much action as development quickens. This MOON rises around noon
   and sets around midnight. She is visible from the time she rises until
   she sets.
4. The gibbous MOON is the bud of the plant, the pulse of life wrapped
   tightly, needing to expand. This is the time to analyze, refine, and
   purify. The gibbous MOON rises mid-afternoon and rests before dawn.
   She is the bulging MOON, ready to be full, visible soon after she rises
   until she sets.

5. The full MOON is the flower, the open blossom, sharing light and beauty to the fullest. There is a desire to enjoy companionship and merge deeply with another. The full MOON rises at sunset and sets at sunrise. She is visible all night long from moonrise to moonset.

6. The disseminating MOON is the fruit of the plant's life cycle, the fruits of wisdom and experience. At this MOON phase, you have much to share and teach. You can live your truth. The disseminating MOON rises mid-evening and sets mid-morning. She is visible in the night sky from the time she rises almost until she sets.

7. The last quarter MOON is the harvest phase, when the plant gives away its life so that others may continue theirs. Now is the powerful reward of the MOON card, the phase of reflection and transformation while maintaining different roles as you skillfully balance your external and internal worlds. The last quarter MOON rises around midnight and sets around noon. She is visible from the time she rises until she sets.

8. The balsamic MOON is the compost phase. Nutrients remain in the soil, providing nourishment for the next new seed. The cycle is complete. Now is the time of insight, patience, and understanding. The balsamic MOON rises before dawn and sets mid-afternoon. She is the last sliver of MOON seen in the eastern sky at dawn and in the very early morning.

To receive the MOON card indicates that you will experience the MOON'S eight-phase cycle. But your outcome is not guaranteed. The plant might not survive. This is not a card of lunacy as some tarot interpretations have claimed, but sometimes in the middle of a MOON change, one may feel a little off-balance. The MOON card is ruled by the mutable waters of Pisces ♓, so try to flow and not become confused or fearful by nebulous Piscean energy. Instead, be open to your intuitive and psychic impressions. (Although the MOON is usually associated with the astrology sign Cancer ♋, in tarot Cancer rules the CHARIOT, not the MOON.)

Both tarot decks depict a portal through which the initiate must pass in order to be transformed. The Rider-Waite deck shows a winding, meandering path, flowing like a river. There will be twists and bends in the road before completion. One experiences evolution into a whole new being, just as the dog evolved from the wolf. A crayfish emerges from the waters; half in water and half on land. These feral animals signify the primality of lunar energy.

Fiery *yods* fall from the MOON in both decks. In the Crowley Thoth deck, mirror images of Anubis, the jackal-headed guide and Lord of Becoming, stand as sentry of the portals. Wild jackal dogs are at their feet. A scarab beetle is shown with a dung ball from which emerges beetle hatchlings, denoting the spontaneous generation of life. *Yods* also fall from the MOON on this deck. The Hebrew letter in the bottom of the MOON card is *quoph*, meaning the back of the hand.

DIVINATORY MEANING:
You are in the middle of a form of evolution. You no longer desire what you did in the past, but you have not yet developed a new sensibility or emotional response. You are unformed, but begin to take on new shape. Events may take more time than anticipated, and the outcome may differ from original intent.

19 · SUN

After the soul is transformed from the inner metamorphosis of the MOON, it can have its day in the golden SUN ☉. The most powerful star in our solar system—around which all the planets revolve—rules this card. The SUN brings energy and vigor, and its daily rising heralds the new day of possibilities and opportunities. The warmth and light of the SUN are vital for almost all life forms. Under this glowing orb, all actions occur during the light of day. There is no darkness or confusion. Instead, there is great clarity. The SUN is often associated with masculine energy, such as the Greek SUN god Apollo and the Egyptian SUN god Ra. But the SUN is also represented by female deities, including the Egyptian goddesses Bast and Sekmet; Irish goddesses Brigid and Etain; Bila in Australia; Aditi in India; and Omikami Amaterasu in Japan.

The Rider-Waite deck shows a SUN with human facial features. Beneath this SUN a radiant joyful child rides a horse and is surrounded by SUNflowers. A large red banner waves upward. The Crowley Thoth deck portrays the SUN with all twelve zodiac SUN signs: Aries the Ram ♈, Taurus the Bull ♉, Gemini the Twins ♊, Cancer the Crab ♋, Leo the Lion ♌, Virgo the Virgin ♍, Libra the Scales ♎, Scorpio the Scorpion ♏, Sagittarius the Archer ♐, Capricorn the Sea Goat ♑, Aquarius the Water Bearer ♒, and Pisces the Fishes ♓. The Hebrew letter on the bottom of the SUN card is *resh*, meaning face.

DIVINATORY MEANING:
Success, prosperity, glory, clarity, and contentment. There is business achievement as well as success in all endeavors. The SUN shines brightly as you radiate strong energy.

20·JUDGMENT *and* 20·AEON

As the victorious soul basks in the SUN, one more transformation occurs, which is represented in the card JUDGMENT/AEON, the card of rebirth. The finest transformation of the soul can occur with this card. The JUDGMENT/AEON card symbolizes a positive rebirth experience less drastic than the DEATH card. The experiences of the JUDGMENT/AEON card are improvement, glory, and joy; and indicate a new life and a new awareness.

In the Rider-Waite deck, JUDGMENT is the glorious JUDGMENT day of rebirth, not the catastrophic JUDGMENT day when one's soul is condemned. This card indicates an opportunity, a new way of being. The archangel Gabriel is shown blowing his trumpet to summon the dead to new life. In response to his call, their coffins open and they are reborn. In your own life, follow the call, follow your bliss. It's not that many are called but few are chosen. Instead, many are called but most refuse. Do not fail to accept your chance to live a rich life.

In the Crowley Thoth deck, the Egyptian goddess Nuit crowns the AEON card. Nuit swallowed the sun each evening to create night and gave birth to the sun each morning to create day. In this way, we too are given the gift of new light in a new AEON, or era. Also on the AEON card, the Egyptian god Horus sits enthroned. The newborn babe represents the Kabbalistic tale that when we are born, we enter life with the knowledge of all things—who we are, what we should do in life, and who we will love. But an angel flies by and touches us on the upper lip, hence the indentation on the face above the lip and below the nose. With the angel's touch we forget everything. It is our life journey to remember again all that we have ever known. The Hebrew letter on the bottom of the AEON card is *shin*, meaning tooth. Three embryos form part of the letter *shin*.

DIVINATORY MEANING

Regardless of your current situation, you are destined to a whole new level of life. It is as if you were reincarnated into a better life experience, but did not have to die and leave the physical body to realize it. The outcome is of a very high order.

21 · WORLD *and* 21 · UNIVERSE

After the rebirth of the JUDGMENT/AEON card is the WORLD/UNI-VERSE, the final card of the FOOL'S journey. All the bounty, wonder, and joy of the WORLD and UNIVERSE is here for us to enjoy. This final card, the pinnacle of all 78 cards in the tarot deck, symbolizes freedom, whole-ness, and attainment. The WORLD/UNIVERSE is ruled by the planet Saturn (Greek Cronos). It required a great deal of time, work, dedication, and discipline to arrive at this final point of the FOOL'S quest. What is completed is strong and long lasting.

Accomplishment in the WORLD cannot be easily snatched away. The Rider-Waite deck shows a victorious female figure draped in purple cloth, dancing within the green circle of life. She holds a wand in each hand. Named the UNIVERSE in the Crowley Thoth deck, this card also shows a figure dancing in the green circle, but she dances with a powerful serpent, symbolic of *kundalini* life force energy. In both decks, the four elements are shown in their fixed modalities: Leo ♌, fixed fire; Scorpio ♏, fixed water; Aquarius ♒, fixed air; and Taurus ♉, fixed earth. The Hebrew letter on the bottom of the UNIVERSE card is *tav* meaning end.

DIVINATORY MEANING:
Realization of the unlimited beauty and wonder of the WORLD. The UNIVERSE is abundant as you dance the dance of life and know fulfillment.

ONLY A FOOL would stop this dance of life and venture out from the green circle of the WORLD/UNIVERSE card. But life is constant change and flux, so the journey begins anew. The cycle of the great round repeats endlessly, as the experiences of the tarot archetypes evolve to new levels of consciousness.

CHAPTER 3:

MINOR ARCANA
FIRE - WANDS

THE 22 MAJOR ARCANA CARDS depict their own unique inner journey. The remaining 56 tarot cards are comprised of 16 court cards and 40 Minor Arcana cards. The 16 court cards rule the four elements: fire, water, air, and earth. The Minor Arcana cards are numbered one (ace) through ten and also are attributed to the four elements. An understanding of the qualities of the four elements is necessary to comprehend the 56 cards of the Minor Arcana.

Recall that the element fire △ rules all things of a fiery nature. In astrological models, Sagittarius ♐ is the mutable (changeable) fire sign; Aries ♈ is the cardinal (moving) fire sign; and Leo ♌ is the fixed (stable) fire sign. In the realm of fire is action, will, drive, creativity, and spirit. In tarot, fire is symbolized by WANDS, rods, batons, or clubs. In a playing card deck, clubs ♣ symbolize fire.

ACE OF WANDS

The ACE OF WANDS is the first card in the world of fire. It combines the qualities of all three of the fire signs; Sagittarius ♐, Aries ♈, and Leo ♌. All ACES represent an element in its purest form, so the ACE OF WANDS is the root of the powers of fire. Also, because ACES are the number one, they represent new opportunity, a new beginning. The ACE OF WANDS image is obviously phallic on both the Rider-Waite and Crowley Thoth decks. In the Rider-Waite image, the sprouting WAND'S leaves fall off in little flames to create the letter *yod*, the first letter of the name of God. The Crowley Thoth deck ACE OF WANDS depicts a mighty giant blazing WAND that emits bolts of lightning. Symbolically, the ACE OF WANDS is the seed of creativity and combustibility. Although the creative spirit has no gender, the ACE OF WANDS most fully expresses the masculine principles of action and power.

DIVINATORY MEANING:
A new door has opened, a marvelous arena to express your creative energies. Utilize passion, strength, enthusiasm, creativity, drive, aggression, and ambition to open the door of opportunity and succeed. Also indicated are love of life, sexual energy, and passion.

TWO OF WANDS

This new beginning leads to the next card: TWO OF WANDS. TWO is the number of partnership, balance, and duality resulting in harmony. The image on the Rider-Waite deck shows a man assessing the world in his hands. How can he develop his domain and establish his will? What must he do to grow, travel, and explore? The key word is *do,* for WANDS represent action. The image on the Crowley Thoth deck TWO OF WANDS is of TWO Tibetan *dorjes,* masculine phallic symbols that represent thunderbolts. Written on the bottom of the card is the word DOMINION, power to rule. The astrological attribute of Mars in Aries ♂ ♈ adds to the powerful, determined spirit. Mars, god of war and courage, possesses the energy to execute new plans. Aries, the first sign of the zodiac that begins on spring equinox, represents the sprouting seed reaching to grow. Mars rules Aries, meaning that the aggressive, dominant, and fiery energies of the red planet Mars are best expressed through the cardinal fire sign Aries.

DIVINATORY MEANING:
Assess your domain and vigorously set goals. Then pursue them with focused attention until they are accomplished and success is attained. The ability to courageously overcome obstacles.

THREE OF WANDS

The THREE OF WANDS combines the element fire with the number THREE, the balance of the trinity. THREE phases of the Goddess are Maiden, Mother, and Crone. Three aspects of a masculine trinity are Father, Son, and Holy Spirit. THREE sides create a pyramid. In numerology, THREE represents both intelligence and humor. The Rider-Waite deck image portrays a man watching boats crossing water, exploring new realms. He is assessing the possibilities available in the world. In the Crowley Thoth deck, the word VIRTUE and the astrological sign of Sun in Aries ☉ ♈ appear on the card. Aries people often act impulsively, then reflect later. With this card, actions are of a pure and noble nature—action in accordance with what is right.

DIVINATORY MEANING:

Rider-Waite: Seeking new adventures and opportunities. Wanting to explore options. Time to find a new way of being.

Crowley Thoth: Proceed with your actions in a virtuous and impeccable manner. Develop integrity and honor. Satisfaction results from carrying out one's duty and fulfilling one's agreements.

FOUR OF WANDS

FOUR is the number of completion and foundation. FOUR OF WANDS represents a completed project or an accomplished goal. The Rider-Waite deck shows two happy people celebrating in front of a castle. The garland of fruits and flowers overhead indicates abundance and harvest. In the background are joyous revelers. On the Crowley Thoth deck is the word COMPLETION, with the astrological attribute of Venus in Aries ♀ ♈. Venus is the goddess of love, so passion with gentleness is required to temper the strong energy of fire and bring affairs to summation. Because these two cards have different meanings, use the meaning for the deck you are using at the time of your reading. With the Rider-Waite deck, observe the celebratory and bountiful energy depicted on the card. With the Crowley Thoth deck, observe the cycle of completion.

DIVINATORY MEANING:

Rider-Waite: Success and prosperity is indicated. Now is the time to finish projects and then celebrate. Complete activities and tie up loose ends.

Crowley Thoth: This card may also mean the end of a romance.

THE WANDS MINOR ARCANA cards numbered TWO, THREE, and FOUR are attributed to Aries ♈ the Ram, cardinal fire. The next three cards are attributed to Leo ♌ the Lion, fixed fire. The last three cards of this suit are attributed to Sagittarius ♐ the Archer, mutable fire. This pattern of cardinal, fixed, and mutable elemental attributes is repeated in all four of the Minor Arcana suits in the Crowley Thoth deck.

The number FIVE represents the suit's element, mired in confusion and chaos. In other spiritual systems, however, the number FIVE can be a very strong and positive number. For example, Chinese Taoist philosophy is built on FIVE elements of fire, earth, metal, water, and wood; an upright FIVE-pointed pentagram star represents the four elements plus spirit; our body is balanced with each hand and foot having FIVE digits; and we possess FIVE senses. But in tarot, all FIVES are cards of problems.

FIVE OF WANDS

Therefore, the FIVE OF WANDS, for example, represents STRIFE. A chaotic battle is depicted on the Rider-Waite deck. There is conflict concerning what to do and how to proceed. Everyone has different purposes, agendas, and methodologies. Crowley attributes Saturn in Leo ♄♌ to the FIVE OF WANDS. The planet Saturn represents hard work, duty, and restrictions. Leo is the ruler of the FIFTH astrological house of creativity, romance, and desire. Hence there are limitations and restrictions on creative expression. The word on the card is STRIFE, which is experienced as STRESS.

Remember that all fire cards symbolize action. The FIVE OF WANDS does not represent restriction of emotions (water), money (earth), nor ideas (air). Instead, the FIVE OF WANDS restriction applies to the ability to take action, to accomplish an intended task, to be able to *do*.

DIVINATORY MEANING:
Competition, chaos, petty problems, and struggle. There are problems concerning what you wish to do. You are held back, imprisoned, or overwhelmed. There is little support for your actions. It is time to check your ego.

SIX OF WANDS

Unlike all the FIVES, which are negative and indicate problems, the number SIX cards are positive and show their element in fulfillment. SIX is balanced, perfect, and harmonious, like a six-pointed star. The place for SIX on the Kabbalistic Tree of Life is the *tiphareth*, the perfect spot of beauty and harmony. The Rider-Waite SIX OF WANDS depicts a triumphant horseman wearing a crown of laurel leaves, the crown of the victor. He is surrounded by admirers. The conflict of the previous card is resolved. Peace is restored. The Crowley deck attributes the planet Jupiter ♃ in the sign of Leo ♌. Bountiful Jupiter, the largest planet, allows for successful and winning actions. The word on the Crowley deck is VICTORY.

DIVINATORY MEANING:
Victorious action, optimism, advancement, positive outcome, recognition or praise, and healthy use of creative energy.

SEVEN OF WANDS

In numerology, SEVEN is a spiritual number, a number of questioning and seeking. In tarot, SEVEN represents inner quest and wondering of a very high order. The Rider-Waite deck shows a person courageously fending off attackers. To continue requires strength and perseverance. Victory may not be worth the battle. The Crowley calls this card VALOUR. It appears as if one can be victorious and determined in action, despite inner doubts and questions. The astrological attribute of Mars in Leo ♂ ♌ shows the strength of both the god of war and the mighty lion. Yet the number SEVEN connotes an inner battle; the lion at war with itself. Perhaps you can maintain a good front and function successfully, but there is not peace within.

DIVINATORY MEANING:

Valour during struggle, striving to stand your ground and maintain your work, yet unsure of your actions. Look within and seek clarity concerning which arena you wish to place your energies, and whether it is best to continue your current projects.

Four is the number of
completion, and EIGHT
is composed of two fours.
When the number EIGHT
is placed on its side, it is
the symbol of infinity.

EIGHT OF WANDS

EIGHT OF WANDS symbolizes action which is part of a completed process, yet also part of an infinite process. We eat and complete the meal, yet we will eat again. We pray, yet prayer is part of an infinite expression. The EIGHT OF WANDS shows activities on the continuum of life experiences. The final three cards of the Minor Arcana suit of WANDS are ruled by the wildfire of the sign Sagittarius ♐. All action occurs and is resolved swiftly. The Rider-Waite deck shows EIGHT WANDS moving quickly across a landscape. In some instances, because the EIGHT WANDS head towards the earth, this can indicate an infatuation that arrives rapidly and leaves rapidly, a flash in the pan. Crowley calls this card SWIFTNESS and attributes it to Mercury in Sagittarius ☿♐. Mercury, the fleet-footed messenger god, quickens the pace and adds enthusiasm to the energy of this card. Also illustrated is a rainbow, a visual illusion of multi-colored light.

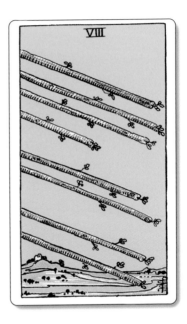

DIVINATORY MEANING:
Life is exciting and fast paced. Events occur serendipitously and quickly. Easy progress. Your world is fun and days seem to melt into each other. Enjoy this whirlwind time.

NINE OF WANDS

NINE is a powerful number. It is three times three, and three added to itself twice. It contains much strength because it is the highest of the single-digit numbers. The Rider-Waite deck shows a defensive man who is on guard, ready to take action and fend off attackers. He anticipates what may happen and holds his own ground. Yet, as indicated by the bandage on his head, he is battle weary. The Crowley Thoth deck differs from Rider-Waite in the interpretation of the NINE OF WANDS. Crowley calls this card STRENGTH and shows NINE victorious arrows with the astrological attribute of Moon in Sagittarius ☽ ♐. The Moon rules emotions, indicating both strength on the emotional level and strength of action. This force includes the integrity of the THREE OF WANDS threefold.

DIVINATORY MEANING:
Strength amidst struggle and integrity amidst adversity. There is willpower and radiance in standing your ground. The ability to fight.

TEN OF WANDS

TEN is the completion of the suit of WANDS. At this peak, there are too many activities that require time and attention, an experience of far too much fire. The Rider-Waite deck shows a figure carrying a backbreaking, overwhelmingly heavy load of TEN WANDS. The Crowley Thoth deck calls this card OPPRESSION, showing fire imprisoned behind bars. The astrological attribute of Saturn in Sagittarius ♄ ♐ is similar to the restrictions of the FIVE OF WANDS' Saturn in Leo ♄ ♌. But in the TEN OF WANDS, the limitations are twice as difficult because Sagittarius cannot bear restrictions.

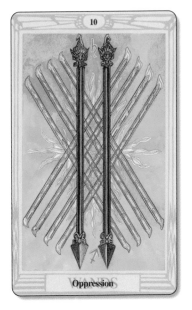

DIVINATORY MEANING:
Overwhelmed with the weight of too many responsibilities and commitments. Prioritize what needs to be done next. Console yourself with the knowledge that because this card is number TEN, the fruition—the burdens cannot increase.

WANDS:
The Court Cards

The suit of WANDS concerns the action-oriented cards of creation, dominion, virtue, completion, strife, victory, valour, swiftness, strength, and oppression. The four court cards are the personification of those who rule this exciting domain.

The QUEEN and KNIGHT are present in both the Rider-Waite and Crowley Thoth tarot decks. However, the two remaining court cards differ.

The Rider-Waite royalty includes a KING and a PAGE.

The Crowley Thoth royalty includes a PRINCE and a PRINCESS.

RIDER-WAITE	CROWLEY THOTH
Queen	Queen
Knight	Knight
King	Prince
Page	Princess

The mature adults of the Rider-Waite deck are the feminine Queen and masculine King. The Rider-Waite adolescent, or unformed, personalities are the masculine Knight and the feminine Page.

The mature adults of the Crowley deck are the feminine Queen and the masculine Knight. The Crowley deck adolescents are the masculine Prince and the feminine Princess.

Court cards may not always match the gender or age of the person using the tarot cards. For examples; If a man receives a QUEEN in a tarot reading, his *anima* (female half) is creative and active. If a woman receives a KING, her *animus* (male side) is activated. If a child appears as a QUEEN or KING, he or she is acting in an adult manner. If adults receive a PAGE or PRINCESS, they may be acting in a child-like manner.

QUEEN OF WANDS
(IN BOTH DECKS)

This proud and strong woman is creative, lively, active, exciting, fun, and friendly. She possesses a magnetic personality and has a sincere interest in the welfare of others. Everyone adores the QUEEN OF WANDS and seeks her companionship. Yet she can exhibit her temper when challenged. A modern American, QUEEN OF WANDS is the Statue of Liberty. Rays of light emanate from her crown as she holds aloft her flaming torch.

Both tarot decks depict a crowned woman on a throne. The Rider-Waite QUEEN OF WANDS holds a large wand and a sunflower, symbolic of the light of the sun. Her throne is decorated with lions and a black cat sits at her feet. Her knees are parted as she sits, the only Rider-Waite QUEEN to do so, indicating sexual energy. The Crowley Thoth QUEEN OF WANDS is seated on a throne of flame and rays flow out from her crown. She also holds a large wand. Her totem animal is a leopard. Because QUEENS are female, they represent the element water, the most feminine element.

The QUEEN OF WANDS
represents the watery
(emotional) part of the
element fire. This
combination of fire's
activity tempered with
water's sensitivity creates a
woman much in demand.
She corresponds to all three
astrological fire signs:
Sagittarius ♐, Aries ♈,
and Leo ♌.

DIVINATORY MEANING:
*Express your creativity and power. Go out and do. Don't
hide your light. Wear the crown and be queen for a day. The
outcome is favorable if you act now with passion, courage,
and brilliance.*

KNIGHT OF WANDS
(IN BOTH DECKS)

This active KNIGHT is on a quest for adventure, action, travel, and excitement. His leaping horse is reared up on its hind legs. The KNIGHT OF WANDS carries a large phallic wand. In the Rider-Waite deck, the wand has sprouted, and in the Crowley deck the wand is ablaze. The KNIGHT OF WANDS represents the fiery (active) part of the element fire, creating a huge blaze. This double dose of fire combines to create an enthusiastic person on the move who is stimulating, passionate, and creative. He corresponds to all three astrological fire signs: Sagittarius ♐, Aries ♈, and Leo ♌, but most specifically to the mutable fire sign Sagittarius ♐.

DIVINATORY MEANING:
The path ahead is clear for dynamic action. Be confident and explore new, fun adventures. Travel is also indicated. This card can represent a sexual explorer who may not be serious about commitment.

Because
KNIGHTS
are male, they
represent the
element fire,
the most
masculine
element.

KING OF WANDS
(IN THE RIDER-WAITE DECK)

This KING is an imposing and brilliant man. He is proud, creative, and acts swiftly. His will is strong and he can rule others with his formidable strength and commanding presence. He is enthroned and holds a large wand, a symbol of fire. With him are animals associated with fire: salamanders and lions. He is responsible, mighty, and a very powerful KING. All KINGS represent mastery, so he is the master of the realm of fire.

DIVINATORY MEANING:
Strength, respect, successful enterprise, and maturity. You are in control. The path ahead is clear for dynamic and victorious action. Success is attained by cultivating and expressing masculine energy.

PAGE OF WANDS
(IN THE RIDER-WAITE DECK)

The youthful and hopeful PAGE OF WANDS is a wanderer and seeker, eager to learn. He sets forth on his journey carrying a large WAND as his walking staff. Good luck is indicated by the red feather in his cap. In the background are pyramids, similar to the KNIGHT OF WANDS card, which indicates travel. Like many born under Fire signs, he is enthusiastic and positive. Due to his youth, he represents new directions of adventure, growth, and exploration.

DIVINATORY MEANING:
Good luck, a new creative cycle, and hope. Learning opportunities and chance for advancement. In some instances, foreign travel is indicated.

PRINCE OF WANDS
(IN THE CROWLEY THOTH DECK)

This PRINCE OF WANDS represents the airy part of fire, intellect and action. He is a warrior in complete armor shown riding a flaming chariot pulled by a lion, the animal of the fire sign Leo ♌. The PRINCE OF WANDS is swift, strong, noble, extravagant, generous, and like all fire signs—a bit impulsive.

DIVINATORY MEANING:

A good time to advance because difficulties are easier to overcome. Goals can be attained, but act swiftly. Courage, winning outcome, ability to perform much work, dedication, and virtue. If you are in a position of power, serve and assist others so that they, too, may gain and increase their good fortune.

PRINCESS OF WANDS
(IN THE CROWLEY THOTH DECK)

She is a sensual, daring, beautiful, and enthusiastic young woman. This character is the original party girl and fun is her middle name. The PRINCESS OF WANDS represents the physical earthy part of fire, the fuel of fire. She is nude and her hair is a huge radiant plume. Next to her an altar blazes as she celebrates.

DIVINATORY MEANING:
Lighten up, dance, and celebrate life. Celebration brings joy and prosperity while healing the heart. Also indicated is spiritual nourishment of self and others.

CHAPTER 4:

MINOR ARCANA
WATER-CUPS

T HE YANG AND MASCULINE ELEMENT FIRE is complemented by the yin and feminine element water. Fire is active and aggressive whereas water is passive and receptive. Water is the element from which life emerges, not only in the evolutionary sense of life evolving from the oceans, but in the concrete sense of life contained in the amniotic fluid of the womb. Water is necessary for life.

The element water $\triangledown$ rules things of a watery nature. In astrological models, water is expressed as mutable (changeable), cardinal (moving), and fixed (stable). Mutable water is Pisces $\mathcal{H}$, cardinal water is Cancer $\mathfrak{S}$, and fixed water is Scorpio $\mathfrak{M}$. In the realm of water is emotion, feeling, psychic ability, and spiritual belief. In tarot, water is symbolized by CUPS. In a playing card deck, hearts ♥ symbolize water.

ACE OF CUPS

The ACE OF CUPS is the first card in the realm of water. The ACE OF CUPS is the root of the powers of water. It combines the qualities of all three water signs; Pisces ♓, Cancer ♋, and Scorpio ♏. The images on both the Rider-Waite and Crowley decks depict the Holy Grail, the womb of life. Both decks depict water lilies, a symbol of purity. The Rider-Waite deck shows the dove of the Holy Spirit with a communion wafer in its beak. The ACE OF CUPS is the chalice of ritual. This card indicates great abundance, fulfillment, fertility, beauty, and pleasure. It manifests as falling in love, feeling vast joy and happiness, or channeling spiritual guidance. In other words, your CUP runneth over.

DIVINATORY MEANING:
A new beginning and opportunity for love, emotional expression, inspiration, and spirituality. Goodness and purity are overflowing.

100

TWO OF CUPS

The river of life flowing from the ACE OF CUPS leads to the next card, the TWO OF CUPS. TWO is the number of partnership, and the Rider-Waite deck shows a loving couple toasting with their CUPS as they pledge their devotion. Above is the caduceus (the wand) of the god Mercury and a winged lion's head. The intertwined serpents of the caduceus are a symbol of healing, hence healing through love. The lion is the red lion of alchemy, symbolic of passion. The Crowley deck shows two intertwined dolphins. The word on the bottom of the card is LOVE with the astrological attribute of Venus in Cancer ♀ ♋. Venus, goddess of love, merges with Cancer, the cardinal water sign of home and mother. The love symbolized by the TWO OF CUPS is nurturing and balanced.

DIVINATORY MEANING:
Love amongst equals, partnership, spiritual union, caring, intimacy, compassion, and harmony. Much time is spent at home because Cancer rules the home and hearth. The Goddess Venus blesses this union.

101

THREE OF CUPS

The THREE OF CUPS brings a new balance. The Rider-Waite deck shows the three Graces toasting and dancing. The pumpkin in the foreground indicates a spiritual harvest, or that emotions will be jubilant come autumn. The word on the Crowley deck is ABUNDANCE, specifically emotional abundance. The astrological attribute of Mercury in Cancer ☿ ♋ indicates easy communication about inner feelings and the personal creative process. Inherent in this card is a sense of safety and protection due to the mothering influence of Cancer. Even though it is a minor card—a little three—it is an important card because the energy it depicts is so lovely, pleasant, and trusting.

DIVINATORY MEANING:

Celebration, merriment, pleasure, rejoicing, and contentment. There are many people with whom you can converse and share your life.

FOUR OF CUPS

The FOUR OF CUPS in the Rider-Waite deck shows a man being offered a FOURTH CUP which he refuses. FOUR is a number of completion, therefore he is full and does not want to receive more. Even though the CUP that is offered is valuable, it is rejected. The Rider-Waite deck indicates "No thank you." In the Crowley deck, the word is LUXURY, meaning excess. The astrological attribute of Moon in Cancer ☽ ♋ is powerful because the Moon rules the sign Cancer. (Those born under the sign of Cancer are often referred to as Moon Children.)

DIVINATORY MEANING:
Rider-Waite: Discontent, boredom, resentment, apathy, lack of enthusiasm. Not wanting what is offered. One is sated and cannot accept any more emotional involvement or entanglement.
Crowley Thoth: Luxury, ease, contentment, and comfort. Flow and harmony.

FIVE OF CUPS

The FIVE OF CUPS represents unpleasant emotions such as pain, loss, and sorrow. The Rider-Waite deck shows a sad, shrouded figure with three CUPS spilled and two CUPS upright. The bad outweighs the good. The hopes of the THREE OF CUPS have been destroyed. Yet two CUPS are still full, and the bridge over the river in the background shows that a new path is not far away. Aleister Crowley attributes Mars in Scorpio ♂ ♏ to this problematic card. The planet Mars rules Scorpio, often leaving Scorpios at war with themselves. A visual theme that runs through the suit of CUPS is the water lily, a symbol of purity, truth, and renewal. But on the Crowley FIVE OF CUPS a decayed lily is depicted with hopelessly knotted roots. The intense inner turmoil occurs below the surface. The word on this card is DISAPPOINTMENT.

Disappointment

DIVINATORY MEANING:
Emotional depression, loss, sadness. Weep and grieve to release the inner disappointments.

SIX OF CUPS

SIX is the perfect number. In the Kaballah number six is the place of Tiphareth. Here beauty, balance, and harmony are located (see page 187). Hence the SIX OF CUPS shows innocent happy children in an idyllic garden of a large home. The children are surrounded by lovely CUPS brimming with flowers. There is a sense of security and protection. Kindness is inherent to this card. The Crowley deck attributes Sun in Scorpio ☉ ♏, meaning passion, depth of emotion, and spirituality. The SIX CUPS are radiant, like illuminated lanterns. The flower roots are strong and golden, unlike the knotted roots of the previous card. There is flow, balance, and symmetry. One can be receptive to life experiences and emotions. Here the pleasure of the THREE OF CUPS is doubled.

DIVINATORY MEANING:
Enjoy life with ease, happiness, and well being. Harmonious giving and receiving. Relationships and emotional states are enjoyable, creative, and sensual.

SEVEN OF CUPS

SEVEN is the number of questioning and wondering. For the suit of CUPS, the questions are: What does one need for emotional fulfillment? How can one fill psychic and spiritual needs? The Rider-Waite deck shows SEVEN CUPS, and SEVEN choices—a beautiful face, a veiled mystery, a serpent, a castle, jewels, a victory crown, and a dragon. Yet these choices are illusions. The word on the Crowley deck is DEBAUCH and shows dank, chipped CUPS. The astrological attribute is Venus in Scorpio ♀ ♏. Venus, the goddesses of love and the arts is playful, whereas Scorpio is shamanic and intense. This combination can be incongruous. Debauchery through alcoholism, drug abuse, and promiscuity only adds to chaos. Inner clarity is required to decide what is real and what is fantasy.

DIVINATORY MEANING:
Unrealistic desires and goals. Wishful thinking. Immature whims, daydreams, and silly imagination. A veil of confusion.

EIGHT OF CUPS

The number EIGHT, symbol of infinity, concerns whether an emotional involvement continues or ends. The EIGHT OF CUPS in the Rider-Waite deck shows a figure walking away from his EIGHT CUPS. He seeks a new path as he journeys towards the mountains. The new moon eclipse indicates a new beginning as the old is left behind. The word on the Crowley deck is INDOLENCE, or laziness. The astrological attribute is Saturn in Pisces ♄ ♓. The planet Saturn restricts the mutable, fluid, visceral Pisces. Mutable signs cannot bear restrictions. The waters of the EIGHT OF CUPS are dark and murky. This can feel like emotional smothering and overwhelm. In most cases, this has been going on for too long a time due to the influence of Saturn.

DIVINATORY MEANING:
You are bored or have lost interest. Rest, heal, and nurture yourself before embarking on a new path. It is best to leave the past behind.

NINE OF CUPS

In the NINE OF CUPS, the magical number NINE combines with the wonderful element water to create HAPPINESS. The harmony and happiness of the THREE OF CUPS are multiplied three times. The Rider-Waite deck shows a well-dressed, contented seated man. NINE CUPS are lined up in an arc behind him. The Crowley deck shows NINE CUPS from which emerge radiant, flowing water. The astrological attribute is Jupiter in Pisces ♃♓. Jupiter is most favorable in Pisces because Piscean sensitivity and psychic ability can expand and flow under Jupiter's benevolent influence. The expansive Jupiter influence of the NINE OF CUPS releases the restrictive Saturn influence of the previous card.

DIVINATORY MEANING:
Happiness, peace, harmony, and contentment. Opportunities and lucky events can occur with ease.

TEN OF CUPS

The TEN OF CUPS is the culmination of the element water. The Rider-Waite deck shows a happy family under a CUP rainbow. Domestic happiness and general contentment are indicated. The Crowley deck shows the TEN CUPS in a Tree of Life pattern. The Kabbalistic Tree of Life is a map of the universe. Every place, or *sephiroth*, on the Tree is illuminated with a flowing CUP. The astrological attribute of Mars in Pisces ♂ ♓ denotes Mars' fierce energy softened by the inherent sweetness of Pisces. Yet the Piscean energy is alive and active under Mars' influence. The word on the Crowley deck is SATIETY, the state of being satisfied. This card is especially fortunate for all types of relationships, especially romance.

DIVINATORY MEANING:
Satisfaction, happy family life, true friendship, and spiritual fulfillment.

CUPS:
THE COURT CARDS

The suit of CUPS concerns the emotional cards of love, spiritual abundance, emotional luxury, disappointment, pleasure, debauchery, indolence, happiness, and satisfaction. The four court cards denote the people who rule this impressionable domain.

QUEEN OF CUPS
(IN BOTH DECKS)

In tarot, all QUEENS represent the element water. Therefore, the QUEEN OF CUPS is the most watery person in the tarot deck. She is an ancient symbol of feminine spiritual force, an omen to connect us to deeper levels of emotion and intuition. The QUEEN OF CUPS is dreamy, romantic, warm-hearted, fair, poetic, psychic, intuitive, and mystical. She makes a devoted wife, loving mother, and caring friend. She can water-gaze for divination. The QUEEN OF CUPS is like a mermaid, studying the inner self reflected in her seashell mirror. In the Rider-Waite deck, she is enthroned at the water's edge, water flowing at her feet. Little mermaid cherubs adorn her throne. She contemplates an ornate wine chalice of the eucharist. The Crowley Thoth QUEEN OF CUPS is gazing at her reflection. Her outward manner is gentle yet she is strong and firm in her resolve. She is enthroned upon still water and is veiled by curves of light.

Her shell holds a crayfish and her totem bird stands beside her. White lilies represent purity, a symbol of the entire CUPS suit. The QUEEN OF CUPS corresponds to all three astrological water signs: Pisces ♓, Cancer ♋, and Scorpio ♏, but specifically Cancer ♋.

DIVINATORY MEANING:
Trust and follow your feelings. Feel the joy of giving and receiving. Be receptive to psychic impressions and dreams. This is a creative time to express inner feeling and unconscious urges, or to nurture oneself and others. Love, peace, and happiness are indicated.

KNIGHT OF CUPS
(IN BOTH DECKS)

In both decks, the KNIGHT OF CUPS carries the Holy Grail, which is a symbol of the womb, the eternal feminine. The Rider-Waite deck shows a chivalrous KNIGHT bearing a CUP. He is imaginative, sweet, and graceful. He is not a warlike KNIGHT, but a poet. All KNIGHTS represent the element fire, so his actions (fire) are tempered with compassion (water) to bring good fortune and healing power. His winged helmet signifies ideas and creative imagination. The Crowley KNIGHT OF CUPS is an angelic man riding a winged white stallion. This KNIGHT carries a CUP, a Holy Grail, from which emerges a crab, the symbol of the astrological water sign Cancer ♋. His animal totem is the peacock, known for its brilliant and majestic florescent plumage.

DIVINATORY MEANING:
If you are stuck or stagnant, he will bring good luck, inspiration, advancement, new opportunities and friends, and emotional fulfillment. He is a spiritual WHEEL OF FORTUNE.

The KNIGHT OF CUPS is a very special KNIGHT because he is the KNIGHT of the grail legend. The story of the grail search is an allegory of seeking truth, beauty, purpose, and salvation in life.

KING OF CUPS
(IN THE RIDER-WAITE DECK)

This KING is a benevolent and generous man of emotional depth and understanding. He is enthroned and holds a scepter in his left hand and a CUP in his right hand. His throne floats on the sea with a ship and a dolphin in the background. The ship indicates journeys into the psychic realm. The sensitive and intelligent dolphin is his animal totem. All KINGS represent mastery, so he is the master of the realm of water.

DIVINATORY MEANING:
Emotional maturity, kindness, and charity. A spiritual or religious person or situation. Consideration for others. The ability to nurture and assist others. Much artistic and creative talent.

PAGE OF CUPS
(IN THE RIDER-WAITE DECK)

The delightful PAGE OF CUPS is a finely-dressed youth who holds a CUP from which emerges a little fish. Good luck, the dream realm, and psychic ability—the small fish indicates creative imagination. In the background is a calm and gentle sea. This image of a young man with a peaceful fish in a CUP brings a sense of joy.

DIVINATORY MEANING:
Good news, happiness, contentment, intuition, and playful creativity.

PRINCE OF CUPS
(IN THE CROWLEY THOTH DECK)

Prince of Cups

This PRINCE OF CUPS represents the airy part of water, intellect and intuition. He is a shaman who rides a nautilus shell pulled by an eagle, the animal of the water sign Scorpio ♏. The eagle symbolizes the Scorpio eagle that flies to great heights with clear vision. In the PRINCE OF CUPS' left hand is a lotus flower, the symbol of purity and truth. In his right hand is a CUP from which emerges a serpent. Because the serpent sheds its skin, it is symbolic of death and renewal. On the helmet of the PRINCE OF CUPS is a phoenix. The imagery is similar to the DEATH card. The characteristics of the PRINCE OF CUPS are subtlety, secrecy, tremendous creative energy, and passion. Scorpio artist Pablo Picasso, born in the year of the serpent, personifies this card.

DIVINATORY MEANING:
Prepare to dive through levels of emotion and peel away what is no longer necessary. This experience is similar to a shaman's death, where reality is transformed and life is viewed with a new, clearer perspective. Sincere feelings, trustworthiness, and integrity of character lead to good fortune and attainment of goals.

PRINCESS OF CUPS
(IN THE CROWLEY THOTH DECK)

Princess of Cups

The impressionable PRINCESS OF CUPS is artistic, dreamy, sensitive, romantic, sweet, tender, kind, and delicately perceptive. Because others may be callous to her endearing qualities, the PRINCESS OF CUPS must take care to not play the role of the victim or martyr. When misunderstood, she could be taken advantage of and abused. She is shown as a dancing figure in a flowing gown, cast about on a wave. Her animal totems are the swan, tortoise, and dolphin. All PRINCESSES represent the element earth, so the PRINCESS OF CUPS integrates the spiritual realm with the material realm, for example in the arts of dance and crafts.

DIVINATORY MEANING:
You are creative, simple, playful, psychic, and a free spirit. Each day is experienced with a child's delight and inquisitiveness. Since this type of person does not excel in the business world, this card can mean victim/martyr roles in the workplace and little financial gain. Watch the tendency to rely on others. Avoid unrealistic fantasies and setting yourself up to fail.

CHAPTER 5:

MINOR ARCANA
AIR - SWORDS

T HE ELEMENT AIR △ CORRESPONDS to the mind, thought, ideas, and intellect. Air is also the wind, the oxygen in our lungs, and the atmosphere of earth. In astrological models, the mutable air sign is Gemini ♊, cardinal air is Libra ♎, and fixed air is Aquarius ♒. (Although Aquarius is the water bearer, it is not a water sign.) In tarot, the masculine element air is symbolized by SWORDS. A SWORD can cut through indecision and confusion to bring clarity of thought, creative insight, and invention. In a playing card deck, air is symbolized as spades ♠.

Unfortunately, the mind is too often filled with worry, doubt, and fear. Or the mind absorbs information that has little to do with the soul's inner workings. Because of this dilemma, most SWORD cards symbolize difficulties. The best solution to dealing with the chaos of SWORDS is meditation to calm and clear the mind. Yoga, deep breathing, chanting, prayer, long walks, and baths also help.

ACE OF SWORDS

The ACE OF SWORDS is the first card in the realm of air. The ACE OF SWORDS symbolizes the root of the powers of air. It combines the qualities of all three air signs; Gemini ♊, Libra ♎, and Aquarius ♒. The Rider-Waite and Crowley decks both depict a magnificent SWORD, a crowned and powerful weapon. In the Rider-Waite deck, a strong hand emerges from clouds, grasping a great SWORD like the Excalibur weapon of Arthurian legend. *Yods* fall from the sky. The Crowley Thoth deck ACE OF SWORDS is crowned in a ring of light.

DIVINATORY MEANING:

Inspiration and epiphany. A new idea or attitude which cuts away confusion. There is clarity of mind, sharp focus, and open communication. Everything is perceived with a different light and expanded consciousness. This could manifest as returning to school, writing a book, or expanding your level of perception.

Ace of Swords

TWO OF SWORDS

The TWO OF SWORDS combines the duality of the number TWO with the abstract mental qualities of air. The Rider-Waite deck shows a blindfolded woman balancing TWO SWORDS as she sits by the sea. Truth will be revealed. Similar to, but less intense than the Major Arcana card JUSTICE/ADJUSTMENT. This card does not mean indecision or pulled in two directions. The Crowley deck shows TWO balanced SWORDS. The word on the bottom of the card is PEACE, peace of mind. The astrological attribute of the Moon in Libra ☽ ♎ denotes a balance of both mind and emotion. When the mind (Libra) is balanced, emotions (Moon) are balanced.

DIVINATORY MEANING:
Peace of mind and harmonious balance. Because this is a "small" card, equal to the two of spades in a playing deck, simply seek peace and do not magnify or overanalyze issues.

THREE OF SWORDS

The THREE OF SWORDS denotes a trinity of pain. The Rider-Waite deck shows a plump heart stabbed with THREE SWORDS under a stormy sky, a vivid image of heartbreak. The Crowley deck shows a flower pierced by THREE SWORDS. The word on the bottom of the card is SORROW, sorrow due to loss, with the astrological attribute of Saturn in Libra ♄ ♎. The sign Libra concerns relationships and partnerships, and Saturn restricts the balance of the Libran scales. Even though this is a minor card, it is deeply felt and imagined. There is a seriousness and gravity to the THREE OF SWORDS as seen in its dark and grave imagery.

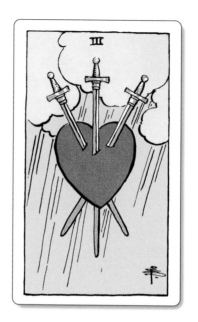

DIVINATORY MEANING:
A broken heart, upsetting emotional relationships, quarrels, and sorrow. It is best to weep, grieve, and release the pain in your heart and mind.

FOUR OF SWORDS

A healing occurs with the FOUR OF SWORDS. FOUR is the number of completion, and with this card the mind can rest after battle. The Rider-Waite deck shows an entombed Knight at rest. One SWORD lies at his side and three SWORDS hang over him. This is not a card of death, but of healing. The stained glass window depicts Christ blessing his followers. The Crowley deck shows FOUR balanced SWORDS and the word TRUCE. The astrological attribute of Jupiter in Libra ♃ ♎ expands the harmony and healing. The lotus flower in the center symoblizes peace and purity.

DIVINATORY MEANING:
Relax and retreat. A truce is declared. No one won, no one lost, and there is no blame. Although there are still issues to be resolved, now there is rest.

123

FIVE OF SWORDS

FIVE is problematic in all of the suits. The FIVE OF SWORDS shows confusion, defeat, and conflict. In the Rider-Waite deck, a stormy sky fills the background. The victor stands in the foreground, while his anguished opponents turn away. They have dropped their weapons in defeat. Conflict is due to differing ideologies, viewpoints, and interpretations. No one can agree. The word on the Crowley deck is DEFEAT, with an image of FIVE twisted SWORDS and bloody tears. The astrological attribute is Venus in Aquarius ♀ ♒. Venus rules love, so this card can also refer to defeat in love relationships.

DIVINATORY MEANING:
You have lost interest or hope. Regardless of how much energy you pump into changing a situation, it makes little difference. Accept your limitations at this time.

SIX OF SWORDS

SIX is the perfect number, (the number of beauty in the Kabbalah), so SIX OF SWORDS is a positive card. The Rider-Waite deck shows a ferryman rowing passengers across the waters of their sorrows to a better place of balance and peace. The Crowley deck shows SIX balanced SWORDS. The word on the Crowley deck is SCIENCE, with the astrological attribute of Mercury in Aquarius ☿ ♒. This is the best sign for Mercury. With the energy of this card, the mind can create solutions to problems, and communicate scientific ideas as tools for discovery and invention.

DIVINATORY MEANING:
A balanced state of mind, healing, calm after the storm, and intelligent communication.

SEVEN OF SWORDS

The SEVEN OF SWORDS addresses the issue of inner battles of the mind. The Rider-Waite deck shows a man stealing away SWORDS like a thief in the night. A military camp is in the background, indicating a state of war. The Crowley deck shows a splintered SWORD, as if the ACE OF SWORDS is shattered. The split SWORD indicates lack of cohesiveness or focus. Ideas are not clear, well thought out, or logical. The astrological attribute is Moon in Aquarius ☽ ♒.

DIVINATORY MEANING:
This card means a weak plan that will fail, and can indicate false friendship. Observe your thoughts, ideas, and belief systems. Root out the destructive thoughts that beget more destructive thoughts.

EIGHT OF SWORDS

The EIGHT OF SWORDS is a card of overwhelming confusion, of too much on the mind. The Rider-Waite deck image is of a woman bound, blindfolded, and encircled by EIGHT SWORDS. She stands in mud, unable to act. The word on the Crowley deck is INTERFERENCE, showing six SWORDS imprisoned behind two other SWORDS. The astrological attribute is Jupiter in Gemini ♃ ♊. Doors open under the guidance of Jupiter, but Gemini is chaotically scattered everywhere.

DIVINATORY MEANING:
Mental overwhelm, exhaustion, and confusion. Obtain clarity about what really requires your attention. Make a list of all the things to do that are overwhelming you, and only do two or three things from the list.

127

NINE OF SWORDS

The NINE OF SWORDS multiplies the grief of the THREE OF SWORDS threefold. The Rider-Waite deck shows a woman haunted by her own sorrowful nightmares. The grief of the NINE OF SWORDS does not emanate from cruelty to others, but rather from self-inflicted wounds. The Crowley deck shows NINE blood-dripping SWORDS. The word is CRUELTY, with the astrological attribute of Mars in Gemini ♂ ♊. Mars, the god of war, battles wildly, and with the mutable air sign Gemini, in a haphazard manner.

DIVINATORY MEANING:
Your mind races with negative thoughts. These thoughts do not come to a final conclusion. Instead, they randomly jab at the soul. Self-torment. Meditation can heal the racing mind.

TEN OF SWORDS

The TEN OF SWORDS is the culmination of the problematic SWORDS. The Rider-Waite deck shows a figure lying face down with TEN SWORDS stabbed in his back. The use of all TEN SWORDS indicates excessiveness. A desolate black sky fills the background. The Crowley deck shows TEN SWORDS and the word on the bottom of the card is RUIN. The astrological attribute of Sun in Gemini ☉ ♊ indicates the scattered and irresponsible, not fun-loving, qualities of Gemini.

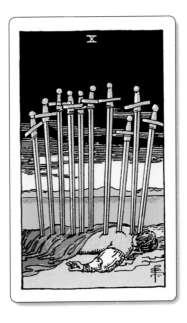

DIVINATORY MEANING:
All is scattered and in disarray. You have made negative choices or you were unreasonable about reality. The end of delusion. Pain. Take comfort that your difficulties will not increase.

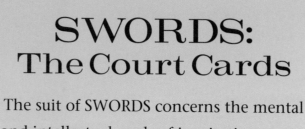

SWORDS:
The Court Cards

The suit of SWORDS concerns the mental and intellectual cards of inspiration, peace of mind, sorrow, truce, defeat, science and invention, futility, interference, cruelty, and ruin. The four court cards are the people who rule this intense and problematic domain.

QUEEN OF SWORDS
(IN BOTH DECKS)

The QUEEN OF SWORDS is a warrioress who can cut away all that is unnecessary. But her approach is not always holistic. Instead she dissects to observe how things work, while not absorbing their totality. In the Rider-Waite deck, she sits enthroned and holds a large SWORD. Storm clouds gather in the background where a bird flies, which is a symbol of air. The Crowley deck QUEEN OF SWORDS is an Amazon who holds a SWORD in one hand and a decapitated head in the other. She is enthroned in the sky and her mind is amplified by crystals. All QUEENS represent the element water, so the QUEEN OF SWORDS represents the watery part of air. This makes her a talented writer and speaker. The QUEEN OF SWORDS corresponds to all three astrological air signs: Gemini ♊, Libra ♎, and Aquarius ♒ (but specifically to the cardinal air sign Libra ♎).

DIVINATORY MEANING:
Control of the mind and thought processes, keen perception, powerful intelligence, clear thought, and liberation of the mind. Traditionally, she denotes a woman (or person) alone, not in a relationship.

Queen of Swords

131

KNIGHT OF SWORDS

(IN BOTH DECKS)

The KNIGHT OF SWORDS represents ideas in action and is shown as a forceful young man. The Rider-Waite deck KNIGHT OF SWORDS is able to fight and defend. He gallops forward with his SWORD drawn and ready for battle. His horse races as a windy storm blows in the background. The Crowley KNIGHT OF SWORDS charges through the sky on his steed. A SWORD is held in one hand while the other hand holds a dagger. He is ready to attack. Three birds accompany him in his swift movements. He represents the fiery part of air, which are both masculine elements, indicating action and inspiration without reflection. The KNIGHT OF SWORDS corresponds to the astrology sign Gemini ♊.

DIVINATORY MEANING:

Methods are too harsh and confrontational. Instead of defiantly defending your position, network, communicate, talk to many people, and orchestrate an open brainstorming situation. Strive to create sharp ideas quickly.

KING OF SWORDS
(IN THE RIDER-WAITE DECK)

This stern KING is a harsh SWORDSMAN. He sits enthroned and holds a huge unsheathed SWORD. Clouds and birds, symbols of air, are behind him. He values the law, judgment, and scientific opinion. He possesses intelligent counsel for matters concerning law, authority, military, educational, religious, and governmental concerns. But he has forgotten his heart and neglects the needs of his body. He is very controlling in a relationship. All KINGS represent mastery, so he is the master of the realm of air.

DIVINATORY MEANING:
Ideas are very focused and directed, but at the expense of the heart. Denotes rational mind, linear thinking, great skill and intelligence with machines and computers. May represent a debater of the law, one extremely intellectual and strongly opinionated.

PAGE OF SWORDS
(IN THE RIDER-WAITE DECK)

The troubled PAGE OF SWORDS stands on shifting ground as he battles the wind in a storm. This androgynous lithe figure gathers all his strength to be on the defensive and prepare to fight. Storm clouds move behind him and a flock of birds form in the distance. He is rash and impulsive, which is not the best way to proceed.

DIVINATORY MEANING:
Trouble ahead, strife, and problems. Instead, try diplomacy and understanding.

PRINCE OF SWORDS
(IN THE CROWLEY THOTH DECK)

This powerful and dark PRINCE is shown riding a chariot pulled by geometric figures. One hand holds up a SWORD, and the other hand holds a sickle, ready to destroy whatever is created. He represents the airy part of air, all intellect and mind, and personifies the astrology sign Aquarius, fixed air. His is the realm of philosophy and science.

DIVINATORY MEANING:
Sharp, focused, and acutely aware. Be clear and consistent. Then you can influence others and, like the wind, penetrate everywhere.

PRINCESS OF SWORDS
(IN THE CROWLEY THOTH DECK)

The angry PRINCESS OF SWORDS battles alone in a dark storm. She attempts to defend a barren altar that is collapsing. She resists change by clinging to negative thoughts, patterns, and judgments. She battles to hold on to the old way, even though it is restrictive and does not apply to the present situation. She represents the earthy part of air, so change is not easy for her. A child of misfortune, she experiences much anxiety.

DIVINATORY MEANING:
Allow your strife, troubles, and worries to collapse. Circumstances will continue to be difficult until you surrender.

CHAPTER 6:

MINOR ARCANA
EARTH -
PENTACLES & DISKS

THE ELEMENT EARTH ▽ RULES ALL THINGS of an earthly nature. In astrological models, earth is expressed as Virgo ♍, mutable earth; Capricorn ♑, cardinal earth; and Taurus ♉, fixed earth. In the realm of earth is the physical body, health, material possessions, career, money, and prosperity. Earth is all of nature, including the planet earth. In tarot, earth is symbolized by pentacles, disks, and coins. A pentacle is a pentagram—a five-pointed star—enclosed in a circle. In a playing deck, earth is symbolized by diamonds ♦.

ACE OF PENTACLES/DISKS

The ACE OF PENTACLES/DISKS is the first card in the realm of earth. The ACE OF PENTACLES/DISKS is the root of the powers of earth. It combines the qualities of all three earth signs; Virgo ♍, Capricorn ♑, and Taurus ♉. The Rider-Waite deck shows a pentacle over a lovely garden with white lilies. The open doorway is an invitation to nature, the realm of earth's beauty. The Crowley deck shows an ornate winged golden coin. This coin sets the tone for the suit of Disks because it is in this suit where we find matters relating to money.

DIVINATORY MEANING:
Wealth, prosperity, gold, a new beginning with material concerns, an increase of money, better health, and financial opportunities.

TWO OF PENTACLES/DISKS

The TWO OF PENTACLES/DISKS represents a CHANGE in the material world. The Rider-Waite deck shows a man juggling TWO PENTACLES united in a symbol of infinity. Ships in the background ride precarious waves. The Crowley deck shows TWO Chinese Taoist yin/yang symbols balanced between a crowned and spotted serpent. The astrological attribute is Jupiter in Capricorn ♃ ♑. Jupiter opens the doors of opportunity. Capricorn, ruled by the serious planet Saturn, understands the principles of hard work.

DIVINATORY MEANING:
Juggling to make ends meet, struggling with the flux of life and the inevitable change in circumstance. This could result in juggling TWO jobs or creating TWO ways to make money. Strive to stay grounded.

THREE OF PENTACLES/DISKS

The THREE OF PENTACLES/DISKS represents the trinity and harmony of the earth plane. The Rider-Waite deck shows a sculptor working in a church that is decorated with THREE PENTACLES above him. A monk is present, representing spirituality. Also present is an architect who holds the blueprint of their project, indicating carefully constructed plans. Good work is being accomplished. The Crowley deck shows THREE whirling wheels. The word on the bottom of the card is WORKS, with the astrological attribute of Mars in Capricorn ♂ ♑. The drive and energy of Mars is best expressed in the practical earth sign of Capricorn. (Occasionally, this card can indicate overwork or just spinning our wheels without any resolution of a project.)

DIVINATORY MEANING:
There is work to be accomplished. Dedicated labor, positive and constructive energy, and completing a task will result in a skillful job well done.

FOUR OF PENTACLES/DISKS

The FOUR OF PENTACLES and the FOUR OF DISKS have different meanings in each deck. The Rider-Waite deck shows a crowned man grasping a PENTACLE, with a PENTACLE under each foot and one on his crown. The Crowley deck's FOUR OF DISKS has the word POWER and the astrological attribute of Sun in Capricorn ☉ ♑. A solid architectural foundation is established with the symbols of each of the FOUR elements in each of the FOUR corners. Fire is △, water is ▽, air is △, and earth is ▽. Note that the divinatory meanings differ. Use the meaning for the deck you are using at the time of your tarot reading.

DIVINATORY MEANING:
Rider-Waite: Love of material wealth, miserly, greedy, fear of financial scarcity, and clinging to possessions. The need to stay grounded and keep what you have. Sensible personal security and good boundaries.
Crowley Thoth: A solid foundation upon which to build. Stability, security, and the ability to create something tangible.

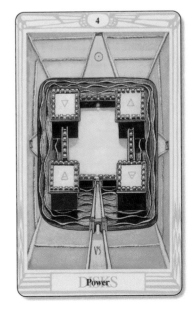

FIVE OF PENTACLES/DISKS

The FIVE OF PENTACLES/DISKS represents problems with money and health. The Rider-Waite deck shows an impoverished couple in a snowstorm. A church with a stained glass window of FIVE PENTACLES is behind them. But the couple does not enter the church. In the Crowley deck, the word on the bottom of the FIVE OF DISKS is WORRY—worry about money and health. The image is a heavy, inverted pentagram. The astrological attribute of quick Mercury ☿ in heavy Taurus ♉ prohibits swift Mercury from creating any change.

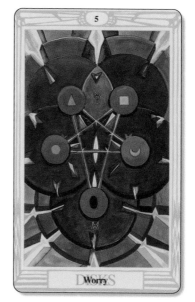

DIVINATORY MEANING:
Lack of money, scarcity, poverty, or bad health. Weak self-esteem. Financial counseling is in order.

SIX OF PENTACLES/DISKS

The SIX OF PENTACLES/DISKS is a card of prosperity and material success. The Rider-Waite deck shows a merchant distributing coins to the poor. He holds a scale, a symbol of balance. He kindly shares his wealth, guided by principles of justice. SUCCESS is the word on the bottom of the Crowley SIX OF DISKS. A balanced mandala is surrounded by symbols of planets. The astrological attribute is Moon in Taurus ☽ ♉, meaning that the sensual qualities of Taurus the gentle bull are best expressed through the receptive emotions of the Moon.

DIVINATORY MEANING:
Business success, prosperity, riches, beautiful surroundings, good health, and abundance.

143

SEVEN OF PENTACLES/DISKS

The number SEVEN is a number of questioning, seeking, and wondering. In the Rider-Waite deck's SEVEN OF PENTACLES, a young man leans on a garden hoe, not yet certain of the outcome of his harvest. Yet much has already been accomplished and steady growth can continue. In the Crowley deck's SEVEN OF DISKS, dark coins are burdened with the astrological attribute of Saturn in Taurus ♄♉. The word on the bottom of the card is FAILURE, with heavy Taurus unwilling to change.

DIVINATORY MEANING:
Projects and endeavors are not yet manifested. Time (Saturn) and hard work (Taurus) are necessary to evolve out of the present scarcity. There may be delay. The harvest or goal is not guaranteed.

EIGHT OF PENTACLES/DISKS

The number EIGHT represents completion or a part of an infinite, ongoing process. The Rider-Waite deck's EIGHT OF PENTACLES shows a craftsman hammering a PENTACLE. The craftsman is almost complete with his project. Six PENTACLES are in place. Only two more PENTACLES need assembling. The Crowley deck's EIGHT OF DISKS shows a flowering tree, firmly rooted and still growing. The word on the bottom of the card is PRUDENCE, with the astrological attribute of Sun in Virgo ☉ ♍. Virgoan qualities are prudence, pragmatism, and attention to detail.

DIVINATORY MEANING:
Steady growth, discipline, and focus. Working towards a goal within your grasp.

NINE OF PENTACLES/DISKS

The NINE OF PENTACLES/DISKS is a card of abundance. The Rider-Waite deck's NINE OF PENTACLES shows a noble figure with a hooded falcon in a lush vineyard. NINE glowing PENTACLES grow on the abundant bushes. The Crowley deck's NINE OF DISKS shows NINE glowing coins. The word on the bottom of the card is GAIN, with the astrological attribute of Venus in Virgo ♀ ♍. This signifies both material gain (Virgo) and increase in beauty (Venus).

DIVINATORY MEANING:
Plenty, success, reward, comfort, financial well being, good management of material affairs, accumulation of wealth, and appreciation of beauty.

146

TEN OF PENTACLES/DISKS

The TEN OF PENTACLES/DISKS is the fruition of all the abundance of the earthly garden. The Rider-Waite TEN OF PENTACLES shows a family; an elderly patriarch at rest, a happy couple, a child, and two white dogs. A stately manor is in the background. The Crowley deck's TEN OF DISKS shows TEN golden coins and the word WEALTH. The TEN glowing COINS are surrounded by many more large thick coins, indicating great abundance and riches. The astrological attribute of Mercury in Virgo ☿ ♍ is very strong because Mercury rules the sign of Virgo.

DIVINATORY MEANING:
Prosperity, security, financial stability, domestic contentment, and riches. Wealth may be increased by detailed attention to communications.

PENTACLES/DISKS:
The Court Cards

The suit of PENTACLES/DISKS concerns the earthly cards of money, financial balance, work, power, worry, success, failure, prudence, gain, and wealth. The four court cards are the people who rule these attributes as well as the creations of nature.

QUEEN OF PENTACLES/DISKS

(IN BOTH DECKS)

This QUEEN is a charming woman who is most at home in the natural world. All QUEENS represent the element water, so she represents both feminine elements of earth and water. She corresponds to the astrology sign Capricorn. In the Rider-Waite deck, the QUEEN OF PENTACLES sits enthroned in a rich lush landscape framed by roses. She holds a large golden PENTACLE. A goat's head on the throne armrest indicates the sign Capricorn. The rabbit in the foreground is a symbol of fertility. In the Crowley deck, the horned and enthroned QUEEN OF DISKS sits by a goat who sits upon a sphere, symbol of Capricorn ♑. She holds a crystal-tipped scepter and a globe as she surveys her landscape.

DIVINATORY MEANING:
Prosperity, wealth, security, luxury, comfort; also charitable and generous. Abundant, fertile, possessing inner strength and dignity. Stable, focused, reliable, practical, talented, and able to exceed in the business world. Understanding the physical body and its pleasures.

KNIGHT OF PENTACLES/DISKS

(IN BOTH DECKS)

This sturdy KNIGHT is slow on his journey. He is the sole KNIGHT whose steed is not in motion. KNIGHTS are male and represent the element fire, the most masculine element. But under the earth influence, the fire is almost extinguished. The KNIGHT OF PENTACLES carries a large golden PENTACLE in the Rider-Waite deck. Unlike the other KNIGHTS, there is little sense of adventure or exploration. In the Crowley deck, the KNIGHT OF DISKS holds a flail and looks down to the earth for his sustenance. He is the only KNIGHT whose steed is stopping to graze. This KNIGHT corresponds to all three astrological earth signs: Virgo ♍, Capricorn ♑, and Taurus ♉, but most specifically to the mutable earth sign Virgo ♍.

DIVINATORY MEANING:
Life is slow, stagnation, lull in activity. The field is fallow. A time to rest. Do not overreach. Powerful endeavors are not favored at this time. You are not ready. Instead, be patient, persistent, dependable, and attend to details. Do not overspend and avoid extremes. It is better to go too slow than too fast.

Knight of Disks

KING OF PENTACLES
(IN THE RIDER-WAITE DECK)

This KING is a reliable, mature, and successful man. He is enthroned in an abundant vineyard in front of his castle. He holds a large golden PENTACLE, symbol of earth. His throne is decorated with bulls, the animal of the earth sign Taurus ♉. In the business realm the KING OF PENTACLES is accomplished and prosperous, he has achieved his goals and attained material wealth. All KINGS represent mastery, so he is the master of the realm of earth.

DIVINATORY MEANING:
You are money-connected, solid as a rock, reliable, and on a strong financial or career path. An experienced and successful leader, especially in business. A reliable marriage partner. This card augers wise financial investments.

PAGE OF PENTACLES
(IN THE RIDER-WAITE DECK)

The youthful PAGE OF PENTACLES slowly walks the lush flowering earth while gazing at the golden PENTACLE in his upraised hands. He is surrounded by an abundant landscape as he seeks earthly guidance. Due to his youth, he seeks new experiences and learning opportunities. This PAGE wears rich garments, especially his fine red hat.

DIVINATORY MEANING:
Desiring to discover and learn how the material world functions; learn how to invest or balance money; interest in health, healing, and nature.

PRINCE OF DISKS
(IN THE CROWLEY THOTH DECK)

Prince of Disks

The steadfast PRINCE OF DISKS represents the earthly part of air, practical intelligence. He is in his natural state as he rides his chariot pulled by an ox, an animal that plows the earth. This PRINCE possesses the qualities of one born in the year of the Ox—solid, reliable, and hard working. His right hand holds a globe and his left hand holds an orbed scepter crowned with a cross. The PRINCE OF DISKS is meditative, capable, competent, slow, persevering, and trustworthy. He is not impulsive or agitated, and does not expect rapid gain. He executes routine, well-planned intentions.

DIVINATORY MEANING:
Solid and reliable in practical matters. Proceed in a patient, orderly way. Progress is made step by step. Calmly follow the correct sequence of events to attain good fortune.

PRINCESS OF DISKS
(IN THE CROWLEY THOTH DECK)

A strong and beautiful PRINCESS is depicted in an enchanted forest. She wears a headdress of horns, a smaller version of her mother's crown (see the QUEEN OF DISKS). The PRINCESS OF DISKS holds a diamond-tipped scepter, pointed downwards to bring spirit to earth. She also holds a rose *mandala* disk, in the center of which is the Taoist yin/yang symbol of balance. The PRINCESS OF DISKS is a young innocent who is open to learning and eager for growth. She represents the earthy part of earth and is very feminine and natural.

DIVINATORY MEANING:
Apprenticeship, new learning experiences, receiving an education, or learning a practical craft or trade. Honesty and sincerity bring good fortune.

You've seen all 78 cards
and read about each one.
Next, the cards come
alive as you apply their
universal archetypes
in tarot card readings.
This is where the
transformation begins!

CHAPTER 7:

HOW TO READ TAROT CARDS

THE DIVINATORY PROCESS is not a random event. All oracles operate on the principle of synchronism. Selecting tarot cards or rune stones, observing the flight of birds, casting a horoscope for the moment of your birth—all involve synchronicity. It is as if we stop life, examine our life with an oracular tool, then return to our normal awareness with an enlightened perception. By skillfully interpreting an oracle, clues to future events become apparent.

To do a tarot reading, start by gently shuffling the tarot cards. Do this image side down, so that the shuffler sees only the backs of the cards. (Shuffle until they feel "cooked," as in baking a cake.) To create sacred space in which to do a tarot reading, refer to Chapter 10 RITUALS WITH TAROT.

After the cards are sufficiently shuffled, cut the cards into three piles as follows: First place the deck on a clean table or flat surface. Then pick up the top two-thirds of the deck, leaving the bottom one-third on the table. With the remaining two-thirds deck still in your hand, cut that into two piles as you move to your right. A prayer may be said over the cards during the three-pile cut, such as "Maiden, Mother, Crone," which are the three phases of the Goddess. Or "Light, Peace, and Serenity," or "Father, Son, and Holy Spirit."

Three piles are now sitting in front of you, each roughly one-third in size. Place the middle pile of cards onto the first one-third pile to your left as you face the piles. Pick up this pile, now two-thirds in size, and place it on the remaining one-third pile on the far right. Now the tarot deck is cut and ready to do a tarot reading. I explain this last step to my students as, "Pick up the Mother, place her on the Maiden, and then place them on the Crone."

If you are doing a reading for yourself, you complete the above procedure from start to finish. If you are doing a tarot reading for another person, they can shuffle and cut the cards in any manner that is comfortable for them. When they are done shuffling and cutting, the reader takes the entire deck from the querent (the one receiving the reading) and the reader does the final three-pile cut as described above.

Traditionally, the tarot card reader asks the querent to shuffle the cards to place some of the querent's energy into the deck. But I do not do this. I do all the shuffling, cutting, and selecting of cards when I do a reading for others. I find that people have trouble shuffling the 78-card tarot deck when they are accustomed to shuffling the regular playing card deck of 52. Also, people usually have a serious concern when they seek advice from the tarot. By doing the complete reading for them they don't have the added stress of having to select the "right" card. As tarot card readers, we are serving the person who seeks guidance from the tarot. Focus on that person, and serve

with as much kindness, gentleness, and understanding that you can.

The first four tarot spreads in this book describe different three-card spreads. To set up the tarot cards to do a three-card spread, shuffle and cut the cards, then take the cut cards face down and fan them out into a big half-moon shape. Then select the cards face down as you intuit them. I prefer to use my right hand since that is my stronger hand, but many prefer the left hand. Use the hand that you prefer.

The Significator

THE "SIGNIFICATOR" is the one special tarot card that most represents (signifies) the person receiving the tarot reading. This significator indicates personal identity and destiny. Its presence during a reading means that particular tarot reading is of greater importance.

Once the significator is determined (which will be explained shortly), *do not remove it from the deck,* and place it first to start your tarot reading. To remove the significator card from the deck does not allow it to surface of its own volition. If you remove it to start, then you are literally not playing with a full deck!

The significator is your personal court card or your personal Major Arcana card. Your astrology sign determines your court card. For example, my court card is the QUEEN OF CUPS because I am a Pisces.

SIGNIFICATOR CARDS AT A GLANCE - ADULTS

	WOMAN		MAN	
	RIDER-WAITE	CROWLEY	RIDER-WAITE	CROWLEY
ARIES ♈	Queen of Wands	Queen of Wands	King of Wands	Knight of Wands
TAURUS ♉	Queen of Pentacles	Queen of Disks	King of Pentacles	Knight of Disks
GEMINI ♊	Queen of Swords	Queen of Swords	King of Swords	Knight of Swords
CANCER ♋	Queen of Cups	Queen of Cups	King of Cups	Knight of Cups
LEO ♌	Queen of Wands	Queen of Wands	King of Wands	Knight of Wands
VIRGO ♍	Queen of Pentacles	Queen of Disks	King of Pentacles	Knight of Disks
LIBRA ♎	Queen of Swords	Queen of Swords	King of Swords	Knight of Swords
SCORPIO ♏	Queen of Cups	Queen of Cups	King of Cups	Knight of Cups
SAGITTARIUS ♐	Queen of Wands	Queen of Wands	King of Wands	Knight of Wands
CAPRICORN ♑	Queen of Pentacles	Queen of Disks	King of Pentacles	Knight of Disks
AQUARIUS ♒	Queen of Swords	Queen of Swords	King of Swords	Knight of Swords
PISCES ♓	Queen of Cups	Queen of Cups	King of Cups	Knight of Cups

SIGNIFICATOR CARDS AT A GLANCE - CHILDREN

	GIRL		BOY	
	RIDER-WAITE	CROWLEY	RIDER-WAITE	CROWLEY
ARIES ♈	Page of Wands	Princess of Wands	Page of Wands	Prince of Wands
TAURUS ♉	Page of Pentacles	Princess of Disks	Page of Pentacles	Prince of Disks
GEMINI ♊	Page of Swords	Princess of Swords	Page of Swords	Prince of Swords
CANCER ♋	Page of Cups	Princess of Cups	Page of Cups	Prince of Cups
LEO ♌	Page of Wands	Princess of Wands	Page of Wands	Prince of Wands
VIRGO ♍	Page of Pentacles	Princess of Disks	Page of Pentacles	Prince of Disks
LIBRA ♎	Page of Swords	Princess of Swords	Page of Swords	Prince of Swords
SCORPIO ♏	Page of Cups	Princess of Cups	Page of Cups	Prince of Cups
SAGITTARIUS ♐	Page of Wands	Princess of Wands	Page of Wands	Prince of Wands
CAPRICORN ♑	Page of Pentacles	Princess of Disks	Page of Pentacles	Prince of Disks
AQUARIUS ♒	Page of Swords	Princess of Swords	Page of Swords	Prince of Swords
PISCES ♓	Page of Cups	Princess of Cups	Page of Cups	Prince of Cups

A woman who is of the fire sign Sagittarius ♐, Aries ♈, or Leo ♌ has the significator card the QUEEN OF WANDS. A fire sign man's significator card is the KING OF WANDS in the Rider-Waite deck or the KNIGHT OF WANDS in the Crowley deck.

A woman who is of the water sign Pisces ♓, Cancer ♋, or Scorpio ♏ has the significator card the QUEEN OF CUPS. A water sign man's significator card is the KING OF CUPS in the Rider-Waite deck or the KNIGHT OF CUPS in the Crowley deck.

A woman who is of the air sign Gemini ♊, Libra ♎, or Aquarius ♒ has the significator card the QUEEN OF SWORDS. An air sign man's significator card is the KING OF SWORDS in the Rider-Waite deck or the KNIGHT OF SWORDS in the Crowley deck.

A woman who is of the earth sign Virgo ♍, Capricorn ♑, or Taurus ♉ has the significator card the QUEEN OF PENTACLES in the Rider deck, or the QUEEN OF DISKS in the Crowley deck. An earth sign man's significator card is the KING OF PENTACLES in the Rider-Waite deck or the KNIGHT OF DISKS in the Crowley deck.

A child's court card is the PAGE of the Rider-Waite deck or the PRINCESS for a girl and the PRINCE for a boy in the Crowley deck. Match the suit to the astrological element, same as an adult. For example, an Aries boy is the PAGE OF WANDS in the Rider-Waite deck or the PRINCE OF WANDS in the Crowley deck. An Aries girl is a PAGE OF WANDS in the Rider-Waite deck or the PRINCESS OF WANDS in the Crowley deck.

No Reversed Cards

SOME TAROT TRADITIONS have special or "opposite" meanings attributed to reversed (upside down) cards. I strongly suggest you avoid confusion and read all tarot cards right side up! If you select a card and it is upside down, turn it right side up and then do your reading.

The meanings of the cards are very clear if you simply study the imagery. For example, FIVE OF PENTACLES/DISKS shows lack of money. So what is the meaning of FIVE OF PENTACLES/DISKS reversed? That would be to *not* lack money. If that were the case, the SIX OF PENTACLES/ DISKS would appear instead, or the ACE. Is the DEVIL reversed the angel of the TEMPERANCE/ART card? Maintain sanity and read all cards right side up at all times, no matter what direction they appear when shuffled.

THE HIGH PRIESTESS.

To determine your personal Major Arcana card, which is your soul card, refer to Chapter 9 TAROT AND NUMBERS. My soul card is the HIGH PRIESTESS. When the PRIESTESS or the QUEEN OF CUPS appear in my tarot reading, I know I am on the right path.

QUEEN of CUPS.

Basic Spreads
BODY-MIND-SPIRIT: A Basic Three-Card Spread

TO GET ACQUAINTED with your tarot cards, discipline yourself to select three cards. Shuffle, cut, and then lay the cards face down, in a semi-circular crescent shape. From this lunar crescent form, intuitively select three cards face down. The first card represents your **BODY:** the material world. The second card represents your **MIND:** thoughts about daily events. The third card represents **SPIRIT:** subconscious guidance and awareness.

If you select three cards in the morning, the day is forecast. If you select three cards in the evening, the day is reassessed.

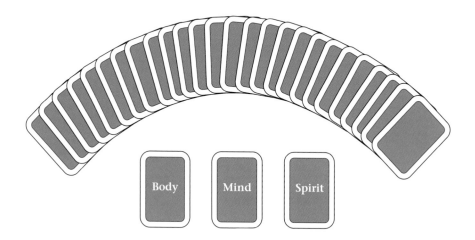

I suggest you keep a daily tarot journal for the first month of your tarot journey, beginning with this Body-Mind-Spirit spread. Study your three cards daily. First identify each card as either *major, minor,* or *court* to better understand them.

The first thing that I say to my tarot students when they begin to read tarot cards is, "Major, minor, or court?" In this way, the student is not lost, trying to remember the meanings of all 78 cards. Remember that a major card indicates a place on the FOOL's journey. Also study the Major Arcana card before and after it to better understand where the card you selected lies in the journey.

A minor card indicates an element. Figure out which element. It will be either fire, water, air, or earth. Note if there is a pattern with numbers.

A court card indicates an element and a personality. Determine a court card's element. Once you know that each of your three cards is either a major, minor, or court card, and know the element of the minors and courts, then proceed with your tarot interpretation.

Major Arcana cards, court cards, and aces are predestined karmic cards of fate. The Minor Arcana cards are indicative of choice, not destiny.

Some three-card spreads will be easier to interpret than others, but soon you will know what it feels like to live the archetypes. Search for a theme, such as the frequent occurrence of a specific card or an overabundance of one element.

When you are comfortable reading this tarot spread for yourself, offer to do the basic three-card spread for others. Either you shuffle or they shuffle the cards, you cut and lay out the half-moon shape, and they can select the three cards face down. If this process flows easily, continue in this manner. (If you try this with someone who has difficulties selecting their three cards, then you will understand why I select the cards for my tarot clients.)

All three tarot cards should be chosen *face down,* and then turned over *only* after all three cards are selected. The reason is that if one card is revealed, the unconscious mind may react to the image on the first card and not be as free when selecting the remaining two cards.

When doing a tarot reading for others, encourage them to focus on their question while the tarot cards are shuffled. Before I read for others, I flip through the cards, showing them the images. I say, "Tarot cards have pictures that tell a story. Some are ducky and some are not so ducky."

You can ask questions to the cards and the pictures tell the tale. Because these are tarot cards, you can be *very* specific. For example, you can ask, "Should I hire A, B, or C?" This little statement should be enough of an explanation to get started.

If the person you are reading for is too shy or embarrassed to tell you their question, reassure them that there are no trivial questions if it is of importance to them. Say that people ask about all kinds of things; relationship dynamics, work choices, spiritual path, health, family issues. Once they understand this, the person will probably feel comfortable offering up their question from the menu you presented. No matter what someone's tarot question may be, you are there to help and serve, not judge and criticize.

Occasionally, a person truly has no specific questions. In that circumstance, I offer to do a general "checkup" on their inner psyche with the Woven Spread (page 194). What is important in their life will surface in the cards.

The issue of whether to read for yourself or others is simple: do both! In rare instances, I've had students (usually Scorpios) who could not read for themselves but were very gifted at reading for others. I recommended that they continue to read for others but barter with another tarot reader for their own readings. Even rarer is the student who can only read for himself and not at all for others. In this circumstance, read tarot cards only for yourself and be grateful that you have a magical tool that directly links you to your spiritual side. As for reading for others, refer them to another tarot card reader.

Tarot *and* Pets

IF YOU WISH TO INCLUDE YOUR PET in your tarot process, willing animals can be trained or gently persuaded to select tarot cards. Shuffle your cards, cut, and lay out the cards in the half-moon shape. Then ask your pet cat, dog, bird, serpent, or other tame animal to place their paw, claw, beak, or body part on three cards. Cats tend to be naturally very acute. Some animals enjoy the process and seek tarot selection opportunities, like my pet parrot Jamilla. She taps her little beak on the back of a card to indicate her selection. She regularly selects the NINE OF CUPS.

Bad News

WHAT TO DO IF BAD NEWS is indicated? You can't deny it since the pictures on the cards clearly tell the story! Instead, plan accordingly. Heal, prevent, or improve a difficult destiny. Life has cycles of high and low, good and bad, day and night. We all face changes in life—the inevitable flow of circumstance, the waxing and waning of opportunities, and the growth and decay of activities. By accepting fate, we can honor continuous life cycles and learn to behave in harmony with universal forces.

But accepting life cycles is not easy for most Westerners to understand. We have been taught that if we control our destiny through drive, will, and ambition, then our fortunes will simply rise forever. It is admirable to be responsible for one's actions and to enjoy the resulting outcome, but life is not always lived in a constant state of only your favorite tarot cards. At times there are cycles of inactivity, roads not taken, and periods of rest that also need to be respected and maintained. The sun does not shine twenty-four hours a day. Nor is it dark day and night. Accept the guidance from the tarot cards. It shows the appropriate cycle of activity for your situation. Even if you do not like the answer that is revealed, the image on the card speaks to your development at this time. Don't keep selecting cards until you get the one you want. Accept what is revealed and meditate on its implications. As I jokingly tell my students, "If you keep picking cards, eventually you'll get the LOVERS."

When you get the same card more than once, pay attention. There are seventy-eight cards in the tarot deck. The chances of a card repeating should be slim, but I often see the same card show up more than one time when I do more than one spread during a tarot card reading session with a client. I also often notice a repeating card theme in my students' homework when they write down their cards for the first month.

Body-Mind-Spirit For Health

TAROT IS NOT A SUBSTITUTE for proper medical care, but tarot can offer insight as to why we experience illness. If someone inquires about their medical problem, shuffle, cut, lay out the half-moon shape and select three cards face down. The first card of the **BODY** can indicate if the illness is purely physical. The answer lies in earth-plane applications such as following doctor's orders, taking herbal medicines, changing diet to eat pure foods, or exercising. The second card of the **MIND** indicates if illness is a result of mental anguish. In this instance, recommend counseling, psychotherapy, and meditation. If illness is indicated in the **SPIRIT** position, shamanic and magical healing such as soul retrieval, past life regression, or hypnotherapy are best to facilitate healing.

This is the spread that I use if someone asks me about weight loss. Usually, the weight loss answer is indicated in the **BODY** position. Interestingly, most diseases are indicated in the **MIND** position. This spread can also be used when asking about the health of someone who is not present at the tarot reading, such as the health of a parent or child.

When it comes to health, common sense is not so common. To lose weight, one must *change* their behavior, regardless of the cards selected. And we humans tend to not like too much change. Here is a health example that required change: A client complained to me about her arthritis. During her reading swords were indicated. She chain smoked cigarettes to calm her racing mind. But the cards also indicated that if she quit smoking, she could start upon a healing path that would eventually include healing her arthritis. She started arguing with me because she didn't want to quit smoking. I decided I simply could not continue reading for her.

Later I wondered if I did the right thing by letting her go and not intervening about her cigarette addiction. So I asked the cards, "Should I continue reading for this client?" I got the HERMIT, which I felt was an affirmation to not read tarot for her anymore.

When someone "acts out" when you read their cards, recommend a therapist to help them process their emotions. As a reader, you must take care of yourself! Too many sensitives and psychics can easily become ill if they allow others to be verbally abusive when the cards don't tell the person what they want to hear. Keep your own Body, Mind, and Spirit clear.

Relationship Three-Card Spread

THIS IS THE MOST POPULAR QUESTION! The basic three-card spread of Body-Mind-Spirit is synchronistically in the present time. A variation

on this three-card format is the prognostic Me-Them-Outcome spread for relationships or any interaction with others. Examples are: you met someone new and wonder if love is in the air and whether you will have a future together. Or you met a new friend and wonder if there is a strong karmic or past life connection or simply whether this is a friendship worth pursuing. Or you just accepted a new job and wish to know the best way to behave, what to expect, and the outcome.

Shuffle, cut, and lay the cards in a half-moon shape. The first card selected face down represents **YOU**: your feelings, thoughts, and subconscious responses to the circumstance. The next card represents **THEM**: the other party involved. The third card represents the **OUTCOME**: for you. Major Arcana cards and aces signify a strong connection. Court cards signify personality types. Minor Arcana cards are important for the element they represent. Look for personal numbers, pairs, matching court cards, harmonious Major Arcana cards, and patterns in the cards to help interpret meaning. For relationships, cups are favored. For work, pentacles/ disks are favored. For a love affair, note that if one person has destiny cards and the other does not, the one without a destiny card may not be as interested.

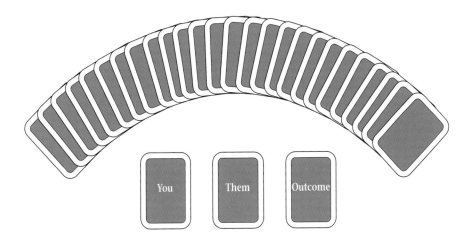

(See explanation of "destiny" cards in next paragraph). Usually, most three-card spreads for relationships show harmonious connections between two people. I often see the NINE OF CUPS, the TWO OF CUPS, LOVERS, and other cards that indicate contentment and compatibility in partnership. (I also cast the horoscopes of both parties to further determine relationship patterns.)

But be prepared to help people who have relationship problems. In many instances, plucky Cupid shoots one person with the arrow of love and the other person with the arrow of indifference. This is indicated when one person has a destiny card and the other does not. A destiny card is represented by a Major Arcana card, court card or an ace (high cards). An indifference card would be represented by a Minor Arcana card (low cards).

For example, a woman asked about a man she was in love with. The first card was the STAR. She was crazy about him. His card was SIX OF PENTACLES/DISKS. He was content to spend the night at her lovely home and enjoyed spending time with her. But his card was far less karmic than her STAR card. Her outcome was QUEEN OF PENTACLES/DISKS. Again, her card was much higher than his card. This was not the news she wanted to hear, but she knew it was true. At least the cards confirmed what she felt.

This Relationship Three-Card/Me-Them-Outcome spread can be used for guidance to help make choices, especially when deciding between two options. For example, if you are dating two people, use one Three-Card/Me-Them-Outcome selection for the first person, and then another Three-Card/Me-Them-Outcome selection for the other person. By comparing the six cards, the choice will be clear. If another party is involved, select three more cards to include information concerning that relationship. This Three-Card/Me-Them-Outcome diagram can also be used when deciding which job offer to accept. Three-Card/Me-Them-Outcome for work choices is very helpful in seeing what the new work environment will be, and for seeing whether the outcome furthers your career path.

Repeating Cards

SOMETIMES MORE THAN ONE card repeats. This was the case when using the Three-Card/Me-Them-Outcome spread about an important competition; the Academy Awards. Two Oscar sweeps were predicted with the same three tarot cards in the same repeat pattern. One of my clients, a film editor in Berkeley, California, asked the cards about the future of the film she was editing. She told me that it was based on a novel and that the film was so stunning, so glorious, that it deserved to win an Oscar. The cards were the SUN, the WHEEL OF FORTUNE, and the MAGICIAN. This combination suggested great good fortune. Her film enjoyed an Oscar sweep.

A year later an artist in San Francisco asked the cards about a film she was doing special effects for. She raved that the special effects alone could win an Oscar. Again I pulled the combination of the SUN, the WHEEL OF FORTUNE, and the MAGICIAN. I told her that in all my years of reading tarot cards, the only other time that this combination occurred was the previous year for an Oscar sweep! Not only would her special effects win, her film probably would sweep too. And indeed, the film *did* win many awards! (As you'll read in Chapter 9 TAROT AND NUMBERS, the number of the SUN card 19 can be added. 1 + 9 = 10. The WHEEL OF FORTUNE's number is 10. Ten can be further reduced since 1 + 0 = 1, which is the number of the MAGICIAN.)

Although your usual tarot card reading may not indicate Academy Awards honors, remember that almost every question to the tarot can be formatted in this Three-Card/Me-Them-Outcome for a clear, precise, and insightful view of many situations.

L'amour, L'amour, Toujours L'Amour
(LOVE, LOVE, ALWAYS LOVE)

THIS BASIC FIVE-CARD SPREAD offers much information to determine the quality of a relationship. It is also interesting to compare the card spreads of the parties involved.

1. What you bring to the relationship.
2. Your future desire in the relationship.
3. What your partner brings to the relationship.
4. Your partner's future desire in the relationship.
5. Why you are together, which also determines how long it lasts and what you can learn.

For example, a woman came to me after she had an enchanting one-night-stand with a musician. She was very excited about how perfect the evening was, how they seemed connected from past lives, and how inspiring and exquisite her lover was. Good for her! But she was emotionally spinning, so we consulted the cards with the Crowley Thoth deck.

1. ART XIV. She chose the very high card of Art and Alchemy (TEMPERANCE in the Rider-Waite deck). The image depicts an alchemical union. Little wonder that she was head-over-heels for a musician who inspired her creativity.

2. PRINCE OF DISKS. For her future, she wanted to move forward, cover much ground, and settle down. This card depicts a Taurus bull (interestingly, the musician was a Taurus).

3. SEVEN OF WANDS. The Minor Arcana card indicated that the musician was not serious. The woman told me that he had two jobs, planned to move, and had many projects that he was working on, so she was not surprised to see this card. It was disappointing to see that her ART card was matched by such a negligible card in this instance. Also, it was not a cup of love, but a wand card of passion and activity. (Generally one hopes to see cups in relationship spreads.)

4. KNIGHT OF DISKS. The musician did not desire a future with her. Instead, he saw the encounter as a dead end, since this is the only Knight not in movement. This was a direct answer to her PRINCE OF DISKS. She wanted future development, but he did not. (I pulled the three other Knights out of the deck to show her how this one Knight indicates stagnation.)

5. AEON XX (JUDGMENT in the Rider-Waite deck). The fact that they even were together, however briefly, was a gift for her. She hadn't been with a man for three years, and this fun encounter was enough to get her juices flowing again.

She realized that to call the musician and chase after him was not a wise idea, even though she was encouraged by her two Major Arcana cards and two court cards. But she kept in mind his SEVEN OF WANDS and behaved maturely.

Past-Present-Future
THREE-CARD SPREAD

A COMMONLY USED SPREAD is yet another variation on the three-card spread. It is called PAST-PRESENT-FUTURE. Shuffle, cut, create the half-moon shape, and then select three cards. The first card will indicate

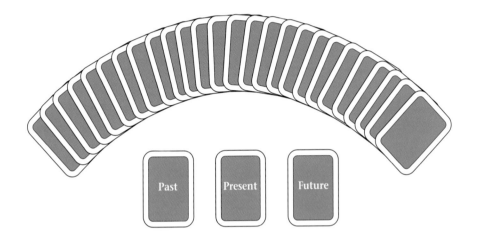

the history of the situation, the second, the present circumstance, and the third card represents what is to come. This is also the spread to use with people when they want to experience tarot for the first time. This spread is fun at parties, fundraisers, and psychic fairs because it is relatively quick—so everyone will have a chance to try it. Whether or not the cards are accurate will be known immediately because everyone knows their past experience.

Many tarot beginners are not trained to understand symbolic language, so they may be embarrassed when the cards reveal their truth. For that reason, it is best to read for an individual in a space that is somewhat private or where others cannot overhear.

If at any time someone is mean to you, ridicules you, is argumentative, disrespectful, or abusive about the tarot cards or your interpretation, simply stop reading for them. You should not have to suffer abuse from others. Remember, too, some people simply cannot perceive the world through metaphorical tarot imagery.

But also be prepared for the opposite to occur. Most people will be fascinated by the tarot, ask you to read for them again, want their friend to try it, and seek to know more about it. When this happens, get a tarot deck for them too and learn together! Watch the magic and blessings unfold as the both of you, or your tarot group, walk the road of tarot and share life experiences as reflected through the cards.

Yes or No - Stay or Go

IN THIS SIMPLE SPREAD two cards can be selected to indicate yes or no. Any either/or choice can be decided in this manner. Shuffle, cut, arrange the cards in the half moon shape, and then select the first card face down to indicate YES and the second card face down to indicate NO. Compare the two cards to determine the best outcome. For example, "Should I vacation in location A or location B?" Decide in advance which location will be card A and which location will be card B. Shuffle, cut, lay out a half-moon spread, and select two cards face down. Then turn them over, upright. The first card indicates location A and the second card indicates location B. Compare and determine which card is most powerful for you. To decide this, look at the picture. The picture will tell the tale. Some will be easy for you to determine, while others will require a deeper look. If doubtful, take your time. Let the cards sit out on the table, and *keep looking.* The answer is within. Even if the card seems negative to you—you still have to look.

A variation on this two-card spread is Stay/Go. For example, the question, "Should I stay in my home or is it time to move?" can be answered in two cards. The first card selected indicates your fate if you stay, and the second card indicates your fate if you go. Again, compare cards to determine the best outcome for your particular situation.

Multiple Choice

IN THE PREVIOUS EXAMPLE, two locations were compared to determine the best place for a vacation. If there were more than two locations, pick a card for each of the locations in mind, and an extra card for "other" (meaning an unknown location that may surface in the future). Be sure to remember the sequence so you do not confuse which card is matched with which location.

In the previous spread, two cards were used to determine whether to stay or go. If "go" is indicated, perhaps there are several locations to be considered. Shuffle, cut, lay out the half-moon shape, and then select the appropriate cards face down, each one representing a specific location. Select an extra card for "other" (which is a location not thought of at the time of the question).

Multiple choice is applicable when a person has many job offers, wishes to choose which creative hobby to pursue, or which college to attend, etc.

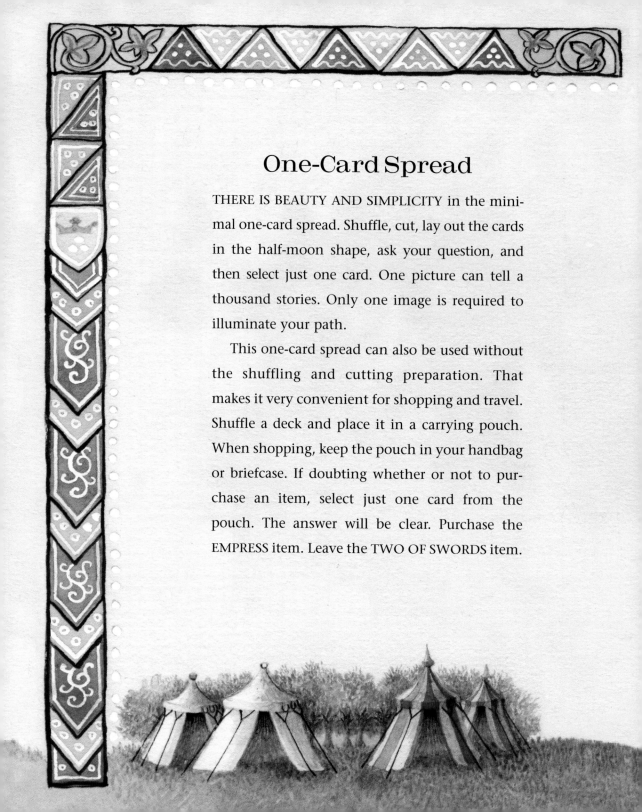

One-Card Spread

THERE IS BEAUTY AND SIMPLICITY in the minimal one-card spread. Shuffle, cut, lay out the cards in the half-moon shape, ask your question, and then select just one card. One picture can tell a thousand stories. Only one image is required to illuminate your path.

This one-card spread can also be used without the shuffling and cutting preparation. That makes it very convenient for shopping and travel. Shuffle a deck and place it in a carrying pouch. When shopping, keep the pouch in your handbag or briefcase. If doubting whether or not to purchase an item, select just one card from the pouch. The answer will be clear. Purchase the EMPRESS item. Leave the TWO OF SWORDS item.

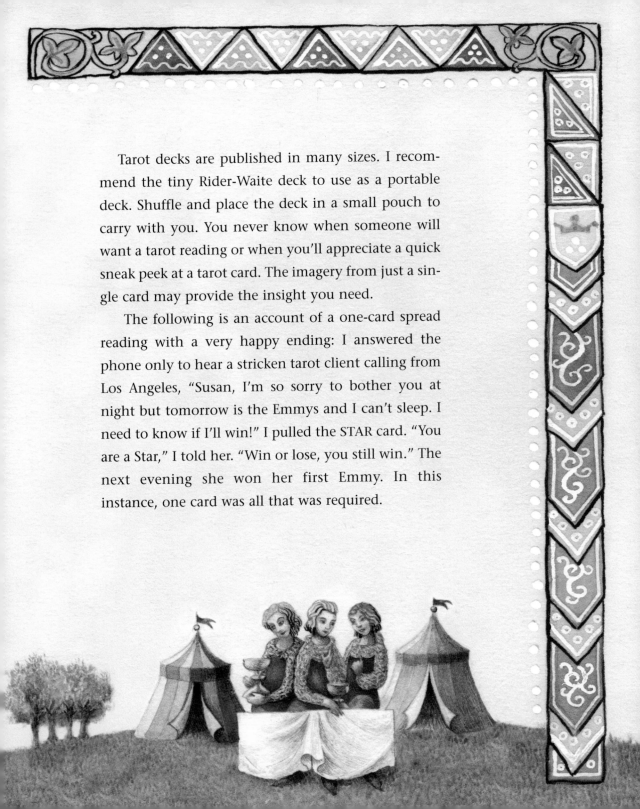

Tarot decks are published in many sizes. I recommend the tiny Rider-Waite deck to use as a portable deck. Shuffle and place the deck in a small pouch to carry with you. You never know when someone will want a tarot reading or when you'll appreciate a quick sneak peek at a tarot card. The imagery from just a single card may provide the insight you need.

The following is an account of a one-card spread reading with a very happy ending: I answered the phone only to hear a stricken tarot client calling from Los Angeles, "Susan, I'm so sorry to bother you at night but tomorrow is the Emmys and I can't sleep. I need to know if I'll win!" I pulled the STAR card. "You are a Star," I told her. "Win or lose, you still win." The next evening she won her first Emmy. In this instance, one card was all that was required.

CHAPTER 8:

SPECIALTY *and* ADVANCED CARD LAYOUTS

Chakra Spread - Seven Cards

STUDENTS OF YOGA and *ayurvedic* medicine may enjoy the SEVEN-CARD CHAKRA SPREAD. Ayurveda means "wisdom of life" in Sanskrit. It is a healing system from ancient India that has been used and refined for thousands of years. The philosophy of ancient Indian culture includes an awareness of the chakras. (Chakra means "wheel" in Sanskrit.) With this tarot spread, a tarot card illustrates the balance in each of the seven chakras. For more information about the chakras, read the Introduction on page 13.

Shuffle and spread the half-moon as described on page 164. Then, select one card for each of the seven chakras. Do not turn them over until all seven are selected. Turn over one card at a time. First note whether a card is major, minor, or court. Majors, courts, and aces indicate more intense action. Do not fear a weak or "bad" card. That only shows you what you need to work on. I find that the fourth card in this spread, the center place of the heart chakra, is an important focus card.

7   **7. INSPIRATION:** How to open yourself in order to receive divine essence

6   **6. VISION:** How to see your highest goal

5   **5. COMMUNICATION:** How to speak with wisdom

4   **4. LOVE:** How to share feelings of compassion

3   **3. POWER:** How to claim personal strength

2   **2. SEX AND CREATIVITY:** How to express yourself

1   **1. SURVIVAL, ROOT:** How to stay grounded

Tree of Life Spread

THE ANCIENT Hebrew mystic system, the *kabbalah,* reveals that each and every person is a star, a container of the light of God. It is as if every individual is a flame, each lit from the same candle. This magnificent light emanates through ten holy attributes that correlate to a number on the Tree of Life. Those who already have a background in this mystical system, or those who would like to learn, might enjoy trying a Tree of Life Spread. The symbolic meaning of the numbers one through ten are the structure of the Tree of Life. Again, shuffle and cut the cards, then place in a half-moon spread

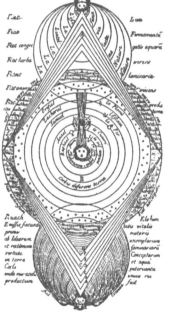

Plan of Kabbalistic doctrine

and select ten cards. In this spread, turn over card 10 *malkuth,* the material realm *first.* End with card 1 *kether,* the crown of divine spiritual light. The tarot cards chosen may not fit into the Tree of Life pattern. For example, an ace may not appear in *kether* the crown, the EMPRESS might not appear in *binah* the mother, and a PENTACLE/DISK may not show up in *malkuth* the kingdom of earth. Note whether cards are major, minor, or court. Look at the suits. Is a suit missing? Are there many of one particular suit? Look for pairs or relationships between the cards, such as court cards of the same element.

1. **One (the Ace)** corresponds to *kether*, the crown of divine spiritual light. *Kether* embodies the energy of absolute unity, the number one.

2. **Two** corresponds to *chokmah*, wisdom and paternal energy, the father.

3. **Three** represents *binah*, understanding, the womb, the primal mother.

4. **Four** corresponds to *chesed*, loving kindness, mercy, and compassion.

5. **Five** corresponds to *geburah*, judgment, strength, and restraint.

6. **Six** corresponds to *tiphareth*, beauty, balance, and harmony.

7. **Seven** corresponds to *netzach*, victory, and dominance.

8. **Eight** corresponds to *hod*, splendor, glory, and submission to God.

9. **Nine** corresponds to *yesod*, foundation, ego, and sexuality.

10. **Ten** corresponds to *malkuth*, the kingdom, the world of action, and the material realm.

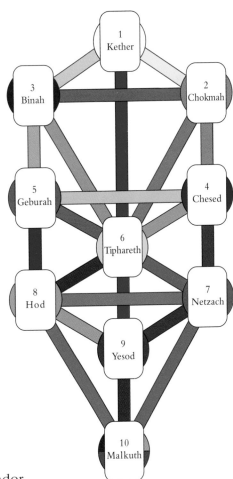

Feng Shui Spread

FENG SHUI is the ancient Chinese art of placement. The nine cards of the feng shui spread match a place on the Chinese map called the ba-gua. *Ba* means eight in Chinese and *gua* means trigram. The ninth card is placed in the middle, the place of balance.

The creation of the eight trigrams is attributed to the legendary Chinese king Fu Shi. A ruler during the ancient Neolithic period of the third millennium B.C., Fu Shi was inspired by the markings on a tortoise shell as the animal emerged from the Yellow River. The eight tortoise shell markings became the eight trigrams of wind, fire, earth, thunder, lake, mountain, water, and heaven. An easy way to remember the eight trigrams is to understand them as the four elements in pairs. Fire is fire and thunder. Water is water and lake. Air is heaven and wind. Earth is earth and mountain.

When you see which ba-gua has a card that indicates something can be done to improve it, take steps to learn feng shui to modify your environment.

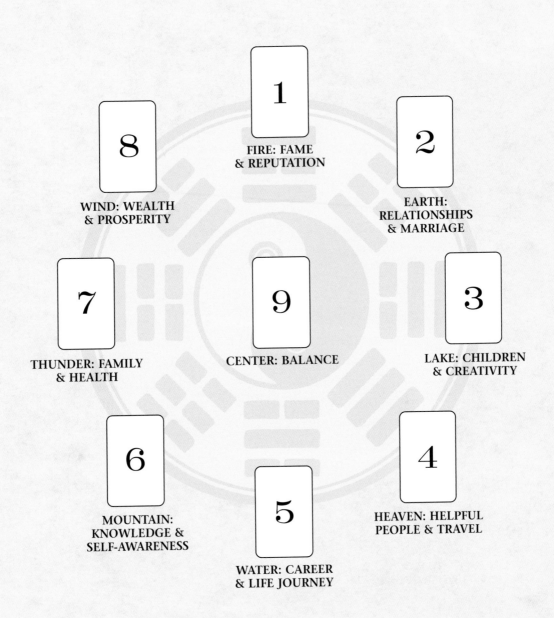

1
FIRE: FAME
& REPUTATION

2
EARTH:
RELATIONSHIPS
& MARRIAGE

8
WIND: WEALTH
& PROSPERITY

7
THUNDER: FAMILY
& HEALTH

9
CENTER: BALANCE

3
LAKE: CHILDREN
& CREATIVITY

6
MOUNTAIN:
KNOWLEDGE &
SELF-AWARENESS

5
WATER: CAREER
& LIFE JOURNEY

4
HEAVEN: HELPFUL
PEOPLE & TRAVEL

CARD 1 – FIRE
FAME AND REPUTATION

This fire card indicates fame, reputation, and respect from others. Bright fire attracts, like a flame for a moth, and can illuminate the way for others. Improvements to this area can bring recognition for your achievements, prominence, clarity, and fulfillment of purpose.

A court card of the WANDS suit, the ACE OF WANDS, or a fiery Major Arcana card, such as the SUN or EMPEROR, is very fortunate in this position because these cards represent the element fire.

CARD 2 – EARTH
RELATIONSHIPS AND MARRIAGE

This card reflects the state of your relationships, especially with your spouse or main partner. Earth is the receptive nurturing feminine principle, so we, too, must be open, receptive, and nurturing to sustain harmonious relationships. Improvements to this area can create more fulfilling relationships, both romantic and platonic, and increase social activities.

Strong PENTACLES/DISKS and harmonious CUPS are well placed here because PENTACLES/DISKS symbolize the element earth, and loving CUPS are desired in relationships. Also great in this position are all cards of healthy relationships such as the Major Arcana cards THE LOVERS and JUSTICE.

CARD 3 – LAKE
CHILDREN AND CREATIVITY

This card position corresponds to children and creativity. Like innocent children playing and swimming safely at a peaceful lake, we can return to our childlike awe to see the amazing world around us. Development of this area encourages you to freely share your creative self-expression, and demonstrate wisdom to compassionately guide children as they grow.

This is the perfect place for CUPS since they indicate feelings. Also good are childlike cards such as THE FOOL, and the ACES, which are cards of new beginnings.

CARD 4 – HEAVEN
HELPFUL PEOPLE AND TRAVEL

This card shows those who assist us in life as if they were angels sent from heaven. This card also indicates opportunities for travel. Enhancements to this area can increase philanthropy, reciprocity in relationships, volunteers, helpful friends, qualified staff, good neighbors, and the ability to find others to assist you when needed.

The TEMPERANCE/ART card personifies this card placement because an angel is depicted on the Rider-Waite deck TEMPERANCE card. Court cards are also desired in this position since they show others who can help you.

CARD 5 - WATER
CAREER AND LIFE JOURNEY

This card corresponds to your career or profession, or journey through life. It is how we flow in the river of life and make a positive contribution through our good work.

If one has difficulties with career or is not doing what is their true calling, enhancement of this area of the ba-gua (in the work place and in the home) may help bring transformation.

Ideal cards here are the MAGICIAN/MAGUS, CHARIOT, STRENGTH/ LUST, STAR, and WORLD/UNIVERSE. Also the ACE OF CUPS which indicates both inspiration and water.

CARD 6 - MOUNTAIN
KNOWLEDGE AND SELF-AWARENESS

This card indicates your knowledge and self-awareness. When we cultivate self-awareness, we can be solid, secure, and as immovable as a mountain. In modern society, the value of meditation, contemplation, and reflection is overlooked. Yet so many personal and social problems would be solved with focused attention on spiritual development. The card here indicates which aspect to develop. If a troubling card appears, it indicates what to understand and overcome.

This is the perfect spot for the HERMIT, the quintessential card of knowledge and self-awareness.

CARD 7 – THUNDER
FAMILY AND HEALTH

The Thunder family card corresponds to family and ancestors. As thunder precedes a storm, our ancestors precede us. This card also indicates health since many illnesses are genetic. Conscientious attention to this area can transform conflicting family relationships to experiences of gratitude, respect, and appreciation for our parents, ancestors, and teachers. This area also corresponds to the balance of power with bosses and managers at work.

The HIEROPHANT is well suited to this position because it can represent the traditional family. Cards that indicate good health, such as STAR and EMPRESS, are also auspicious in this position.

CARD 8 - WIND
WEALTH AND PROSPERITY

This card corresponds to wealth, prosperity, and blessings—as if good fortune will arive on gentle winds. The gifts from this area are wealth, prosperity, harmony, abundance, receiving honors, and promotion. Development of the wind position can increase opportunities for making and receiving money, expansion of a business, and good luck.

Obviously, high pentacles/disks cards that indicate prosperity would be ideal here (such as the ACE OF PENTACLES/DISKS or the TEN OF PENTACLES/DISKS) though certainly not the FIVE OF PENTACLES/DISKS, which indicates poverty. Very lucky is THE WHEEL OF FORTUNE since FORTUNE is present.

CARD 9 - CENTER
PLACE OF BALANCE

It is in the balance of all eight cards that we find harmony, peace, and contentment. The ninth card shows how to tie it all together, and what to strive for in the tarot reading. There is no "best" card here. Whichever card appears is what you are meant to integrate into the totality of your being. Good or bad, bitter or sweet, that is your next life lesson.

In this Feng Shui Spread, each card does not exist in isolation from the others. There is reciprocity between all areas of life experience. For example, the earth-relationship card is important if a marriage partner is desired. But it is also important to study the mountain-knowledge card. If you know yourself, you can create a strong relationship with another. If the wind-wealth card shows abundance in your life, give to others to become their heaven-helpful person.

The Woven Spread

THE WOVEN SPREAD is my favorite all-purpose ten-card tarot spread. It is the spread to use for a comprehensive tarot reading when a client does not have a specific question. It is also perfect for birthdays and new year readings, and for a relationship reading that is more in-depth than the Three-Card/Me-Them-Outcome or the L'amour, L'amour, Toujours L'amour spreads.

The woven spread is a variation of the Celtic cross pattern. In the woven spread, each tarot card builds upon and weaves meaning with the previous card. To begin the woven spread, shuffle and cut the cards. Instead of laying out the cards in the half-moon shape, take the first card off the top of the pile. Lay it face up, right side up. Lay out all ten cards one at a time face up. In this instance, it is fine to see the card's face because the reading will use the first ten cards in the pile, regardless of your initial response. Look at the cards. Think major, minor, or court. Which elements are present? What is the response in your body, your gut feeling? What is your mind's response when analyzing the cards? What is your spirit's response, your intuitive sense? Look at the cards a bit more, and then begin your tarot interpretation.

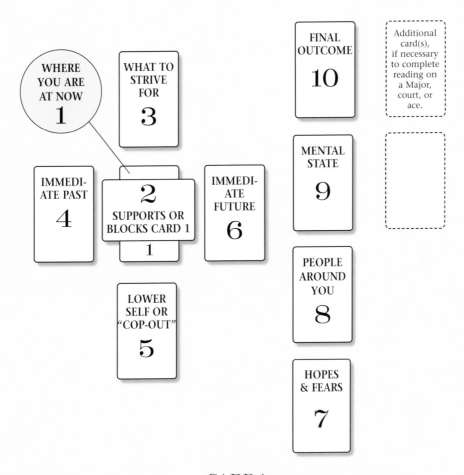

CARD 1:

Shows where you are now. Much information can be ascertained by contemplation of this one card. Observe whether it is a court card, which shows an aspect of your personality; a Major Arcana card, which shows a predestined place on the FOOL'S journey through the archetypes; an ace that indicates a karmic new beginning; or a Minor Arcana card, which shows the important element in your life right now.

CARD 2:

Shows what either supports or blocks card 1. If this card is at cross purpose with the first card, the conflict is clear. An example of this is if card 1 is JUDG-MENT/AEON crossed by card 2, the NINE OF SWORDS. In card 1, Rebirth is occurring, but card 2 denotes that the mind refuses to release old patterns to allow for new growth. Conversely, a harmonious combination is two cards that blend well together or are of compatible elements. For example, if card 1 is TWO

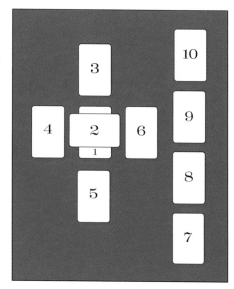

OF CUPS and card 2 is the STAR, these cards blend nicely.

CARD 3:

Is placed above card 2 and shows what to do. This is the crown card that blesses your tarot reading. Strive to develop the qualities of card 3. If it is a pleasant card, such as the TEN OF CUPS, it may be easier to cultivate those qualities than if card 3 were a problematic card, such as the FIVE OF SWORDS. But the FIVE OF SWORDS may be necessary to experience, not deny, to facilitate growth and evolution. This card in this third position is for your highest good.

CARD 4:

Is placed at the left of the first two cards and shows your past. Observe the meaning of this card and see how it brought you to cards 1 and 2. When you see the imagery, you will know if it refers to the immediate past or the general past. In most instances this card indicates immediate past.

CARD 5:

Is placed on the bottom and shows what NOT to do. This is the "cop out" card, how you may tend to run away and hide, or deny what is taking place in front of you. Try to attain the heights of card 3 and not cultivate the qualities of card 5 (even if it is a very favorable card).

CARD 6:

Is placed to the right of the first two cards and shows the future. Read straight across the four cards of card 4 (past), cards 1 and 2 (present) and card 6 (future) for a basic prognostic PAST-PRESENT-FUTURE insight. Guidelines for behavior are given in card 3 (crown) and card 5 (cop out). Reading across 4, 1, 2, and 6 is considered an embellished form of the PAST-PRESENT-FUTURE three-card spread.

CARD 7:

Begins at the bottom of the row and indicates hopes and fears. This card may be the most important card of the reading because our hopes and fears can be unconscious urges that block our true path from unfolding. For example, we hope for love, yet on some levels we may fear love. We may hope for success, yet we may fear it. Compare card 7 to the future card 6. Does the energy of card 7 assist with the future? Does it relate to the issues of the past in card 4? Does it support the energy of the crown card 3? Or does it meet below with the energy of card 5 and focus on the wrong thing? Does this card 7 of hopes and fears support or deny the present circumstances of card 1 and 2? Start weaving the meanings of the cards when you interpret the meaning of card 7. Look for patterns; major, minor, court, element, and numbers.

CARD 8:

Is placed above card 7 and shows your environment and the people surrounding you. If the tarot reading concerns a relationship, card 8 shows how the other person in the relationship feels about you. In a tarot reading about work, card 8 indicates how other employees see you, as well as the general atmosphere at work. If a court card appears in the card 8 position, it represents another individual—not you—who personifies that court card. Otherwise, all court cards in the other positions of the woven spread are aspects of yourself, not other people.

Weave the meaning of card 8. Observe if your environment supports your goals of cards 1, 2, 3, and 7. Perhaps they activate the energy of the cop out card 5, or place you back into the past of card 4. If card 8 indicates that others are experiencing struggles, decide whether to assist them or to separate. Or if card 8 shows that all is well around you, reach out for help or be at peace that you have appropriate surroundings that don't require your fixing.

CARD 9:

Is placed above card 8 and represents your mental state, or attitude, about the reading. A positive mental balance can help a seemingly poor card 6 of the future. An upsetting card 9 can negate the power of the other cards, so notice how the mind can influence the outcome.

CARD 10:

Is placed above card 9 and represents the final outcome. This will come to pass in about one month's time, or one full lunar cycle. Again, weave meaning. Observe the journey from the past, card 4, to the destination of card 10.

The 10th or final outcome card must end on a card of fate: a Major Arcana card, a court card, or an ace. In this way, the journey is complete on a card of destiny and power, not a less significant Minor Arcana choice card. If a Major Arcana, court card, or ace does *not* appear in the card 10 position, keep laying cards in another row to the right until there is a solid resolution of a destined ending. The Minor Arcana cards laid until a destiny card appears are the minor ups and downs experienced until reaching the final conclusion. Observe the numbers, elements, and time frame. Each extra minor card laid out represents one month of time, although wands, especially the EIGHT OF WANDS, indicate a shorter time segment.

The woven spread cards are laid out in a counter-clockwise position, meaning that one is not bound to this reading. Instead, one has the power to embellish a positive destiny or intervene to improve a difficult destiny. The first six cards in the circle represent feminine energy. Cards 7 through 10 in a straight line represent male energy. This side by side placement of circular and linear shapes can create an insightful tarot interpretation.

WOVEN ONE-YEAR *and* BIRTHDAY SPREADS

IF THE WOVEN SPREAD is to last one year, or is done on a birthday to prognosticate the upcoming year, the influence of cards 1 and 2 will continue for a couple of months. Card 4 represents last year. Card 6 will endure for the first six months. Card 9 will be obvious in about nine month's time. The final outcome card will manifest during the last three months of the year. Cards 3 and 5 will be valid throughout the entire year. If more than ten cards are used until a destiny card ends the reading, modulate the time sequence to include these Minor Arcana experiences.

CHAPTER 9:

TAROT *and* NUMBERS

EVERYONE HAS THEIR OWN PERSONAL Major Arcana tarot cards in addition to their Significator. These cards have greater impact when they appear in a tarot reading. Personal cards are determined by adding the numbers of your birth date in a column. For example, my birth date is March 15, 1955 (3/15/1955):

$$
\begin{array}{r}
3 \\
15 \\
+1955 \\
\hline
1973
\end{array}
$$

Then add 1973 across: 1+9+7+3=20. (1+9=10, 10+7=17, 17+3=20.) The number 20 can be further reduced: 2+0=2.

Of the 22 Major Arcana cards numbered FOOL 0 through WORLD 21/UNIVERSE 21, card 20 and 2 are JUDGMENT/AEON 20 and PRIESTESS 2 respectively. JUDGMENT 20/AEON 20 is the card of my personality, what I project to others, and what others see. Similar to the rising sign of astrology, this is my persona, or mask. Although people may see the transformational process of JUDGMENT 20/AEON 20, the real me behind the mask is determined by the single digit number 2, the PRIESTESS. I identify with the PRIESTESS because she is who I am (a professional tarot reader, astrologer, and feng shui consultant). My hobbies are studying traditional Chinese medicine, writing, and reading. The archetype of the PRIESTESS lives through me.

The column method of adding birth numbers is used for tarot. It differs from traditional numerology which deems me an 11, a number of high spiritual vibration. In classical numerology, my birth date 3/15/1955 is added as 3+1+5+1+9+5+5=29. Add 2+9=11. Hence, I am an 11, which does not reduce to 2 because 11 is considered a master number in classical numerology, and therefore is not reduced.

Examples of Tarot and Numbers

MY YOUNGER SISTER CHAR, my soul mate, demonstrates another example of finding the personal Major Arcana cards as an archetype to live by. She was born June 5, 1958 (6/5/1958). Therefore:

$$
\begin{array}{r}
6 \\
5 \\
+1958 \\
\hline
1969
\end{array}
$$

1969 is broken down as follows: 1+9=10; 10+6=16; 16+9=25. But 25 is not represented in the 22 Major Arcana cards. Therefore, add 2+5=7, the CHARIOT. In this example, there is no double-digit persona card, only a single digit soul card. Since the personality and soul cards are one and the same, Char is a double CHARIOT. She is an athlete and a manager where she works. It is obvious to those who know her that she is a warrioress who can move through all obstacles. In classical numerology, 7 is the number of the spiritual seeker, which also suits her.

Add the birth data of family, friends, and co-workers to see which Major Arcana cards they embody. Recall that all numbers that are higher than 22 will reduce to just a single digit for both the personality and soul, as in Char's example.

Number 22 is attributed to the FOOL. That would reduce to number 4, the EMPEROR. Therefore if one's birthdate reduces to 22, their persona is the FOOL and their soul is the EMPEROR.

When the birth numbers add up to 19, this is the only instance where three Major Arcana archetypes are activated. The birth date of February 3, 1976 (2/3/1976) is figured as follows:

$$
\begin{array}{r}
2 \\
3 \\
+1976 \\
\hline
1981
\end{array}
$$

Add 1981: 1+9=10; 10+8=18; 18+1=19. The Major Arcana card 19 is THE SUN. Then add 1+9=10. The Major Arcana card 10 is the WHEEL OF FORTUNE. Finally add 1+0=1. The Major Arcana card 1 is THE MAGICIAN. These three numbers of 19 SUN, 10 WHEEL OF FORTUNE, and 1 MAGICIAN are a lucky and winning combination.

Addresses *and* History

THIS SYSTEM OF ADDING NUMBERS to discover a Major Arcana correlation has myriad uses. The energy of a building can be determined by adding the numbers of the address (do not include apartment/suite numbers or the zip code). For example, 111 Fifth Street would be figured 1+1+1=3, the EMPRESS. Excellent for a lovely place to live. Historical dates can be understood in their Major Arcana correlation. For example, March 12, 1519 (3/12/1519) was the date that the ship of the Spanish explorer Hernando Cortez landed near Vera Cruz, Mexico:

$$\begin{array}{r} 3 \\ 12 \\ +1519 \\ \hline 1534 \end{array}$$

1+5=6; 6+3=9; 9+4=13, the Major Arcana card DEATH. 1+3=4, the Major Arcana card the EMPEROR. That fateful day could only reduce to the DEATH 13 card and the EMPEROR 4 card. The domination of Spanish colonial rule was a personification of the EMPEROR and a DEATH for the way of life for the indigenous peoples of Mexico.

Personality *and* Soul Cards: Magician·1 *through* Hermit·9

STUDY THE PERSONALITY AND SOUL CARDS of your friends and relatives (personality cards are double-digit cards, while soul cards are single digit cards). It is especially insightful for parents and caregivers to know their children's Major Arcana cards to best determine the natural path for their child's growth and development.

MAGICIAN·1/MAGUS·1
(Also present are WHEEL OF FORTUNE 10 and SUN 19)

The soul of a MAGICIAN is independent, original, a leader, and a self-starter. The dynamic power and vitality of number 1 can be transformed to the highest healing alchemy using the magical tools of the MAGICIAN. Cultivate a path of spiritual development and study the magical arts. Maintain a positive attitude by valuing the many talents and abilities with which you were born.

With the personality cards of the SUN 19 and the WHEEL OF FORTUNE 10, this indicates a charmed life. This person will have the soul of the MAGICIAN who can work magic and make all will-powered events come true. Their personality shows the radiant success of the SUN after the ever-revolving WHEEL OF FORTUNE turns in their favor. Doors of opportunity can open easily because the SUN and the MAGICIAN have the power to make the best of any situation.

PRIESTESS · 2

(Also present are JUSTICE/LUST 11 and JUDGEMENT/AEON 20)

The PRIESTESS 2 soul, like all soul numbers, can belong to either a female or male.

The soul of the PRIESTESS is expressed through love, service, peace, gentleness, harmony, and quiet meditation. The PRIESTESS blossoms with a simple life dedicated to metaphysical work. Cultivate a peaceful environment away from the limelight. The total bliss of *samadi* (unity of body, mind, and spirit) is available to the PRIESTESS who walks the inner path of spirit and service without thought of reward. The PRIESTESS 2 soul, like all soul numbers, can belong to either a female or male.

The personality number of JUSTICE 11 signifies one who values honesty and integrity. With the LUST 11 Major Arcana card, the enthusiasm and creativity of the lustful persona can be guided with the insight and wisdom of the PRIESTESS soul. If you do not know whether your 11 personality number is JUSTICE or LUST, look to your horoscope. Planets in Libra, or being born in the year of the Dog, indicate JUSTICE. Planets in Leo or fire signs indicate LUST.

With the 20 persona and 2 soul numbers, the JUDGMENT/AEON persona can set an example through inspirational activities and know that their personality has a transforming and healing effect on others.

EMPRESS·3

(Also present are HANGED MAN 12 and WORLD/UNIVERSE 21)

The soul of the EMPRESS is most highly expressed through joy, talent, and humor. Appreciate beauty, cultivate artistry, develop creativity, and you will reap a full harvest. The EMPRESS 3 soul can enjoy the loveliness of nature, secure that the abundant universe provides all of life's necessities.

With the persona of the HANGED MAN 12, there may be false starts, dead ends, and minor frustrations in life. But when the inner garden of the EMPRESS 3 soul is cultivated, trials can be endured with grace. The Buddhist concept of, "Chop wood, carry water"—and then after enlightenment one *still* chops wood and carries water—applies to the HANGED MAN 12 persona.

The persona of the WORLD/UNIVERSE 21 is very blessed because the UNIVERSE is so abundant. If this is your card, the WORLD is your oyster. You can live your dreams because the EMPRESS 3 will manifest them. The EMPRESS 3 soul can harvest what is destined to be hers.

The abundant universe provides all of life's necessities.

EMPEROR · 4

(Also present are FOOL 0 [22] and DEATH 13)

The soul of the EMPEROR 4 excels in a realm that he can control. He does best when running his own business or doing work which does not compromise his ideals. The EMPEROR needs to be a leader, not a follower, even if the only person he leads is himself. He should avoid situations where others supervise him as he works. The EMPEROR 4 enjoys stability, trust, and perseverance with the even number 4. But he needs to express those qualities in a vigorous manner. Participation is the key to the EMPEROR'S happiness. This archetype is a powerhouse, so be conscious that the energy is used for healing purposes, not to dominate others.

The persona number of 22 indicates the FOOL 0. This allows for the EMPEROR to take creative risks. Most freelancers and entrepreneurs have this FOOLish EMPEROR combination. If the persona card is DEATH 13, pursue fascinating experiences of transformation and deep insight. Hypnotherapy, trance states, shamanic journeys, or working with the dying are hobbies or professions that are satisfying to the DEATH 13 persona.

HIEROPHANT·5

(Also present is TEMPERANCE/ART 14)

The soul of the HIEROPHANT grapples with the inner issue of whether to conform to societal structure or rebel against cultural limitations. The choice of whether to follow the rules or devise a new system is the creative challenge for the HIERO-PHANT 5 soul. Therefore a dichotomy exists. Should the HIEROPHANT 5 acquiesce to the expected role, or strike out against the established social order? During a HIEROPHANT'S lifetime, they will experience both. HIEROPHANT types often work traditional jobs in structured environments such as offices, law firms, medicine, or academic environments.

Yet they want to bring a new way to the old traditions. In classical numerology, the number 5 indicates one who is restless, loves travel and adventure, is versatile, and needs freedom.

With the persona card of TEMPERANCE 14/ART 14, this gifted and inspired person excels by becoming an artist or developing an artistic outlet. They can transform their life like an alchemist, creating gold out of base metal. Even under the most challenging of circumstances, especially during a hard childhood, the TEMPERANCE 14/ART 14 personality can rise above all obstacles to make a better life.

LOVERS · 6
(Also present is DEVIL 15)

The soul of the LOVERS 6 has one task in life: self love. When we love ourselves, we can mirror that love through others. To heal the earth, we can start by healing ourselves. The LOVERS 6 soul can integrate many expressions of love to feel connections to all forms of life—be they human, plant, animal, or elemental. In the Native American tradition, this connection is referred to as "all my relations." Six is an even number of harmony, balance, and peace. Cultivate peaceful moments for meditation and relaxation. Six also symbolizes responsibility and dedication.

With the persona of the DEVIL 15, one must strive to retain personal power, especially in partnership. There may be a tendency to create codependent or controlling relationships. Another danger is to be too influenced by messages of popular culture, the media, or fads. Consuming the latest styles and crazes, or imitating mainstream dictates, will not lead to your truth.

Six is an even number of harmony, balance, and peace.

CHARIOT · 7
(Also present is TOWER 16)

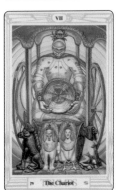

The soul of the CHARIOT 7 has a sense of life purpose and direction, regardless of external circumstance. They are spared existential dilemmas about the nature of existence. The CHARIOT 7 soul can focus their energy, walk a strong path for their spiritual development, and perform useful work that contributes to society. Seven is a spiritual number of seeking, questing, analysis, and intuition, which keeps the CHARIOT 7 moving.

The persona of the TOWER 16 may seem like a problematic personality card, perceived as experiencing many difficult or intense transformations. Regardless of obstacles, the soul of the CHARIOT 7 knows who they are and where they are going. The TOWER persona is well suited for travel to sites such as Tibet, Stonehenge, Machu Picchu, Chaco Canyon, the Nile River, Delphi, the Yucatan peninsula, and other sacred locations.

Seven is a spiritual number of
seeking, questing, analysis, and intuition.

STRENGTH · 8 *and* ADJUSTMENT · 8
(Also present is STAR 17)

In classical numerology, 8 represents power, money, and success. This holds true for the STRENGTH 8 card as well as the ADJUSTMENT 8 card. The STRENGTH 8 card is ruled by the sign Leo. This is your soul card if you are a Leo or have Leo and the other fire signs Sagittarius and Aries dominant in your horoscope. The STRENGTH soul is fortunate to be naturally gifted with courage, perseverance, fortitude, and a powerful will.

The ADJUSTMENT 8 card is ruled by the sign Libra. This is your soul card if you are a Libra, or have Libra and the other air signs Gemini and Aquarius dominant in your chart. Mental clarity, peace of mind, and fairness in thought and deed are valuable attributes of the ADJUSTMENT 8 soul.

People with the STAR 17 persona are literally born under a lucky Star. They are often popular and radiate energy. The STAR 17 persona is both beautiful and brilliant.

HERMIT · 9
(Also present is MOON 18)

The soul of the HERMIT 9 can successfully cultivate a quiet life of contemplation, rich inner development, and meditation. The HERMIT 9 soul has the ability to find peace in solitude. It is important to have private time separate from others, or to pursue solitary hobbies or interests. Nine is also the number of universal love and humanitarian principles, so HERMIT 9 souls are interested in a variety of metaphysical subjects.

The persona card of the MOON 18 signifies a personality that is always in a state of change and growth. This persona manifests as one who doesn't easily decide their spiritual path or life direction. What was once appropriate at a certain age may not still hold true later in life. Often this type is shy and tends to withdraw during a cycle of change. After they finish their cycle, they are much more social. With such a strong lunar influence, a MOON 18 persona is very intuitive, psychic, and impressionable—a natural tarot card reader! The HERMIT 9 soul is an excellent complement that allows the ever-changing MOON 18 persona to withdraw, meditate, and evolve.

Tarot, Numbers, *and* the Current Year

EACH YEAR WE TRAVEL THROUGH the Major Arcana tarot cards. To determine your personal year, add your birth month and birth date to the current year. For example:

$$
\begin{array}{r}
3 \\
15 \\
+2001 \\
\hline
2019 = 12. \quad 1+2=3
\end{array}
$$

Add 2+0+1+9=12. Add 1+2=3. I am experiencing an EMPRESS 3 year. I am very content experiencing a 3 year because I strongly identify with the EMPRESS.

IN A ONE YEAR, the year of the MAGICIAN 1/MAGUS 1, is a new beginning, the start of a nine-year cycle. This year is a powerful time of creativity, fortune, and lucky opportunities.

IN A TWO YEAR, the year of the PRIESTESS 2, one can find romance because two is a number of partnership. A two year is also a peaceful time to focus on the activities initiated on the previous year.

IN A THREE YEAR, the year of the EMPRESS 3, there is activity, enjoyment, celebration, growth, and perhaps travel. Depending on individual temperament, some enjoy the three year while others find it a hectic or nervous time.

IN A FOUR YEAR, the year of the EMPEROR 4, it is a time of work and focus. Like the two year, even-numbered years are best for cultivating stability whereas odd-numbered years encourage change.

IN A FIVE YEAR, the year of the HIEROPHANT 5, it is a good year to travel, move, set up a new home, and try new things. The influence of the HIEROPHANT 5 offers a steady hand.

IN A SIX YEAR, the year of the LOVERS 6, it is a time to cultivate beauty, peace, inner balance, and harmony in your life. There is love and partnership like a two year and disciplined work like a four year.

IN A SEVEN YEAR, the year of the CHARIOT 7, one questions the meaning of their existence and desires to know why they are doing what they are doing. The seven year is the time to question theology, career choice, and relationships. The CHARIOT 7 moves forward after inner questions are answered.

IN AN EIGHT YEAR, the year of STRENGTH 8 and ADJUSTMENT 8, it is a time of power, fame, and money. Answers from the previous year are focused and manifested to create success. For the soul card STRENGTH 8, one is experiencing strength and power. For a soul card ADJUSTMENT 8, it is best to stay balanced during this time of success. Like all even numbers, in an eight year there is stability.

IN A NINE YEAR, the year of the HERMIT 9, the cycle ends. This is the time to complete projects, spend time alone, and release all things that no longer serve your highest good. Clean out the old. Prepare for the next year's new beginning when the MAGICIAN/ MAGUS arrives.

CHAPTER 10:

RITUALS WITH TAROT

FOR THOUSANDS OF YEARS, rituals and ceremonies were conducted during new and full moons. As the moon changes and grows, we change and grow. As above, so below.

The new moon is an excellent time to do a tarot card reading for yourself and others. It is a time of new beginnings and a fresh start for your creative potential. Insights from a new moon tarot reading can help establish goals for the upcoming lunar cycle. The new moon represents the goddess in her maiden aspect.

Or you may prefer to do tarot readings on a full moon when lunar energy is at its peak. The full moon is a time of illumination and reflection on what was accomplished since the new moon. The full moon represents the goddess in her mother aspect.

The dark moon is a time of banishment and purging. Tarot cards may be consulted at this time to understand the wisest path of surrender and release. The dark moon represents the goddess in her crone aspect.

I recommend doing a full woven spread tarot card reading on the new moon, the full moon, or both. Also on your birthday (your solar return), the New Year, Chinese New Year (the second new moon after winter solstice), the two equinoxes, the two solstices, and whenever a circumstance arises which requires divination.

The spring and fall equinoxes are a time of balance, which are excellent periods to address the tarot with questions concerning balance and harmony. The summer and winter solstices are extremes of light and dark. Therefore ask the tarot for guidance about life direction and to validate choices. If you are unable to set aside time for a tarot reading on these important days, note the day in some manner, no matter how small, intimate, or personal. For example, place fresh flowers in a vase on spring equinox, or light a small candle for the winter solstice.

Rites *of* Earth
Blessed Art Thou, Creatures of Earth

PRIOR TO READING YOUR TAROT CARDS, physically clean and purify your element earth—your home. Assess the room where you read your tarot cards by pretending that you are a guest entering your home for the first time. What do you see? What do you smell? What do you hear? And most importantly, how do you feel? Data and research cannot tell you why you feel calm in one place and uneasy in another place. It simply cannot be explained in words. Instead it is simply known and felt. It is intuition—that little bit of human instinct, a direct wisdom that is an important part of working with tarot cards.

Clean your home with the mindful intention of transforming your environment into a sacred space. Clean until you feel calm and centered. Sweep or vacuum and remove clutter. Clean untidy messes, pick up clothes from the floor, clean the bathroom, and wash the dishes. Wash mirrors and windows. (Cleanliness is next to god/goddessliness.)

How you maintain your home can determine your health, wealth, quality of relationships, luck, career development, fortunate opportunities, self-cultivation, and creativity. The ancient Chinese Taoists created the art and science of feng shui (pronounced "fung shway"). Feng shui means wind and water, two elements of nature that can shape mountains.

When doing your tarot card readings, never indulge in any drugs, alcohol, or stimulents such as cigarettes, coffee, and caffeinated beverages. Intoxicants of any kind cast confusion when reading cards.

To relax your body, have a healing massage, chiropractic alignment, or acupuncture treatment a day or two prior to doing a tarot reading. Your body is your physical temple, so exercise, sleep, and a healthy diet of wholesome foods is important to maintain emotional balance and equilibrium so important to spiritual work. If you find that tarot readings drain your energy, get more sleep. After a ten-hour or twelve-hour deep sleep, you will be refreshed and able to continue.

Inside the deep womb of Mother Earth lie many beautiful and powerful mysteries of creation. One of her mysteries is the power of crystals. They have a life of their own and, like us, are alive. Using crystals with tarot can enhance and amplify your tarot interpretations. Crystals are highly evolved minerals and are very sensitive. Their sensitivity sets them apart from other rocks. Clear quartz crystals bring clarity. Dark stones, such as smoky quartz crystal or obsidian, can keep you centered if you become dizzy or flighty while doing a tarot reading. Rose quartz helps to open your heart for compassionate tarot readings. Amethyst crystal aids in opening the third eye to develop clear psychic vision. If you use just one stone, amethyst may be the best choice overall.

The various shapes, sizes, colors, and textures of crystals correlate to the energies of the sun, moon, and planets. As above, so below.

1. SUN ☉ crystals protect and heal. Diamonds are clear and radiant like the sun. Red stones, such as garnet and ruby, contain solar energy as do golden topaz and amber, a fossilized tree resin. The corresponding Major Arcana card is, of course, the SUN.

2. MOON ☽ crystals release and clarify emotions. Lunar stones are moonstone and opal. Pearls, a gift from the sea, are also lunar. The corresponding Major Arcana card is the MOON.

3. MERCURY ☿ crystals enhance communication. Clear quartz crystals shaped like wands, especially the double-terminated wand shape, and clear crystal clusters serve this purpose. The corresponding Major Arcana card is the MAGICIAN/MAGUS.

4. VENUS ♀ crystals are beautiful and can harmonize energy. Rose quartz, emerald, citrine, tourmaline, peridot, and jade are all stones of Venus. The corresponding Major Arcana card is the EMPRESS.

5. MARS ♂ crystals focus and direct energy. These powerful stones include carnelian, bloodstone, malachite, red jasper, and tiger's eye. The corresponding Major Arcana card is the EMPEROR.

6. JUPITER ♃ crystals expand energy and inspire. Jupiterian stones are lapis lazuli, amethyst, sapphire, and azurite. The corresponding Major Arcana card is the WHEEL OF FORTUNE.

7. SATURN ♄ crystals concentrate and manifest energy. These stones are black tourmaline, jet, smoky quartz, and obsidian. The corresponding Major Arcana card is the WORLD/UNIVERSE.

8. URANUS ⛢ crystals connect us with other galaxies. Azurite, chryso-prase, and chrysocolla are Uranian in nature. The corresponding Major Arcana card is the FOOL.

9. NEPTUNE ♆ crystals are used as tools in meditation. Blue stones of sapphire, aquamarine, turquoise, and blue topaz are Neptunian, as is coral. The corresponding Major Arcana card is the HANGED MAN.

10. PLUTO ♇ crystals can transform energy. These include Herkimer diamonds, rutilated quartz, tanzanite, and chalcedony. The corresponding Major Arcana card is the DEATH card.

Rites *of* Air
Blessed Art Thou, Creatures of Air

AIR IN OUR BODIES is our breath. To invoke air, focus on your breath. Relax your muscles and experience a meditative state. In this quieter state, slow your body rhythms and mental percep-tions. Feel your breath inhaling and exhaling. Listen for your heart-beat, your internal drum of life.

As you breathe, you inhale the fragrances around you. Our intu-ition is influenced by smell. When you enter a dwelling and the air is foul, your response is to want to leave. If the air is sweet or inviting, you immediately want to stay. Realtors will bake bread or cookies in a home right before an open house because they know how the sense of smell effects people. Every human prefers the fragrance of roses and jasmine to the stench of pollution and smoke. For that reason, incense and scented oils have been used in religious ritual for millions of years. If you go to church and smell frankincense, an incense made from tree resin, right away you will feel a deeper connection to god. The scent of incense in an ashram will help you attain a peaceful state.

The magic of scent can transform your environment in preparation for a tarot card reading. Open a window or door and burn a purifying incense. These include frankincense and myrrh, sage, rosemary, copal, cedar, and sweetgrass. The classic incenses of frankincense and myrrh can be combined to create a sweet-smelling fragrance. Frankincense represents the sun and myrrh represents the moon. Myrrh added to any incense strengthens its powers.

If you do not have access to those incenses, burn the kitchen herbs of rosemary or sage. Fragrant rosemary was used during the Middle Ages in Europe to ward off the plague and mask the stench of the dead.

The kitchen herb sage is used by Native Americans as a strong cleanser and purifier. Sage can be burned alone or in combination with cedar. After the sage is burned to cleanse, sweetgrass can then be burned to leave a fresh and sweet aroma.

To burn herbs, place them in an ashtray or other safe container, light them, and fan the smoldering herbs. They will burn easily if fanned. As the herbs burn, walk through your rooms and fill them with scented smoke. (You could also experiment with other herbs such as bay laurel leaves and lavender.)

As you carry the smoking herbs and incenses, they will fill your rooms with a pleasant scent. Pay special attention to corners and behind doors. If doing a tarot reading outdoors, allow the smoke to freely fly up to the skies or be carried away on the wind.

If someone has allergies or is chemically sensitive, they

might feel ill from any type of incense smoke. In this circumstance, use an aromatherapy diffuser available at health food stores. The diffuser is used with essential oils. Use the best quality essential oils you can find. A good scent to start with is lavender. Calming scents are derived from the oils of most flowers and fruits, including chamomile, rose, orange, and grapefruit. Healing scents are derived from the oils of clary sage, juniper, and eucalyptus. I use the aroma spray Orange Mate in my home before tarot clients arrive. Orange Mate cleans the air, is an uplifting scent, and does not aggravate allergies.

Rites *of* Fire
Blessed Art Thou, Creatures of Fire

FIRE IS ILLUMINATION. Nothing is brighter than fire. To introduce the element fire into your environment, employ the art of candle magic. All candles work regardless of shape. Just be sure that your candle burns safely. I often use little white tea light candles in ceramic containers, which are very safe. White candles are recommended for all magical work because white represents spiritual purity and moral goodness. If you are new to candle magic, start by burning a white candle for light, peace, and serenity. Light the white candle and begin your tarot reading. I simply say, "Blessed art thou, creature of fire" while lighting.

After your tarot reading, allow the candle to burn all the way down and extinguish itself, or extinguish the flame yourself with wetted fingers or a candlesnuffer. When a candle burns itself out, the energy of the tarot reading continues. The benefit of a candle that is snuffed out is that the candle may be used again for the next tarot

223

card reading. Do not blow out a candle, which disperses the flame. Remove wax from a candleholder by soaking it in hot water. The wax will come off easily.

Another way to introduce the element fire is to use beeswax candles. These candles are very pure, unlike other candles which are made from a petroleum base. Beeswax candles are naturally a dull honey color, although you can find beeswax candles that have been dyed other colors. Sometime they are coated with bee pollen dust. The flame of beeswax candles is larger and clearer than the flames of petroleum based candles. The burning beeswax emits a natural sweet honey scent. When beeswax candles are extinguished, they do not have a harsh smell like other candles.

Candle colors other than white are used for their symbolic meaning. There are three primary colors: blue, red, and yellow. These colors exist in a pure state in nature. All other colors are derived from blends of these three primary colors.

- BLUE CANDLES represent peace (like white) and spiritual healing. Blue is a restful color for meditation and contemplation. Blue also corresponds to the element water.
- RED CANDLES add strength, vitality, and passion. Red represents the element fire, thus a red candle brings a double dose of fire. (Use red candles sparingly because they are very powerful.)
- YELLOW CANDLES are used for mental clarity, communication, and truth. Yellow corresponds to the element air.

Combining the three primary colors creates the three secondary colors: green, purple, and orange.

- GREEN is a combination of blue and yellow. Green candles are used for wealth, prosperity, and physical healing.

- PURPLE is a combination of blue and red. Purple candles are used for success, power, and royal countenance.
- ORANGE is a combination of red and yellow. Orange candles are used for life, vigor, and protection.

Tertiary colors are created by combining three or more colors. Tertiary colored candles are not as focused as primary colors, but do have their purpose in candle magic. Brown candles are used for solidity and to represent the earth. Turquoise and lavender candles are high spiritual candle colors that evoke blessings. Adding white to a primary color softens it: pink and light blue are candle colors for love.

Black is the color of deep transformation and shamanic perception. Black candles are not recommended for beginners. A small black or gray candle may be appropriate for winter solstice to represent the dark of night. A black candle may be burned next to an orange candle on Halloween. The black candle represents the dead and the orange candle represents the living. Otherwise, avoid black candles unless you are deliberately seeking shamanic states. One client complained that she always hosted awful dinner parties. Her silver candelabra with eight black candles was lit at every meal. When she changed to golden beeswax candles, her guests enjoyed the warm glow. When in doubt, use white or plain beeswax. Can't decide what color to use? Shuffle, cut, lay out the half-moon shape and select one card face down for white, another card face down for beeswax, and another card for the alternate color under consideration. Go with the card you prefer.

Discard pillar candles when they are used up, or if they burn lopsided. Also discard candles in glass containers that burn black soot on the glass. Replace with fresh candles instead of re-lighting a sooty stub.

Rites *of* Water
Blessed Art Thou, Creatures of Water

TO INTRODUCE THE ELEMENT WATER, set out a glass of water for you to drink while you do your tarot card reading. I also have a glass of water prepared for my clients when they come to my home for a tarot reading. Each glass contains spring water and a slice of organic orange in the water to flavor the water and make it more refreshing. I make sure that my client drinks their entire glass of water during the hour-long tarot reading. (My advice to my clients is to always drink plenty of water!)

After a tarot card reading, I usually bathe in a tub of scented herbs, mineral salts, or clay to offer prayers and release the energy of the client's issues. If I have many clients in a row, I wash my hands before and after each tarot reading. You may wish to bathe prior to a reading to remove any psychic impressions that might block your ability to be clear with the tarot cards. If you do not bathe beforehand, be sure to bathe or shower afterwards to let the water wash away any residue from the reading.

Water is a great healer. When you take your scented bath, you can add a few drops of essential oils that are appropriate for you. Or you can add Epsom salts to the bath water. These inexpensive salts are available at most drug stores. Epsom salts draw out body toxins and send them down the drain. You can even add baking soda to your bath water for a soothing effect. Or you can make a concoction of herbs that soothe skin, such as chamomile and comfrey. If very uncomfortable or intense interactions occurred during a tarot card reading, afterwards take a long swim in a pool, or walk by the ocean or another body of water. This will help flush away the energy of the reading.

Another way to add water to your tarot life and enhance your psychic abilities is to use flower essences, a technique pioneered in the 1930s in England by Dr. Edward Bach. Flower essences are not scented like aromatherapy essential oils. In fact, many have no scent at all. Flower essences contain life force energy from plants, and flower essences are made by releasing the vibrational qualities of a flower into water. They heal the aura, open higher chakras, and are superb for developing balanced sensitivity. To use, a few drops of flower essence water is placed under your tongue or diluted in a glass of water. It is best to take them before sleep at night. Emotional healing occurs during the first two hours of sleep.

Two outstanding brands of flower essences are Bach flower essences and California flower essences. I have given the Bach flower essence "Oak" to help weak souls become strong as an oak tree. For nervous types, I recommend the Bach flower essence derived from the plant "Vervain." Over the years, I have recommended the all-purpose Bach flower essence "Rescue Remedy" for tarot clients' pets that are experiencing trauma.

It is very easy to use California flower essences to help develop psychic skills. I read the California flower essence booklet to decide which essences were right for me. Quite a few applied, so I brought my tarot deck to a health food store where they were sold and pulled tarot cards for each of the essences. I purchased "Fawn Lily," which was the STAR card, and "Easter Lily," which was the QUEEN OF CUPS. I also recommend the STAR brand flower essence "Pink Lotus" to help one recognize the judgments they may have and to open their heart to compassion.

How to Treat Your Tarot Deck

YOUR TAROT CARDS ARE A MAGICAL TOOL to be highly regarded, not left lying on the floor or thrown into a drawer. A respectful approach is essential.

When you receive a new tarot deck, that first night place the deck in the bed with you as you sleep, perhaps under the pillow. Have a pen and paper next to your bed to jot down any or all things remembered during your dream state. You may wish to carry your tarot deck with you for the next few days to become familiar with it.

There are many different views on how to store your tarot cards when they are not being used. Traditionally, tarot decks are wrapped in silk to protect them. Silk is perhaps the most amazing fabric in the world. Silk is made from the cocoons of silk worms that feed on the leaves of mulberry trees. It is soft, dyes and drapes beautifully, and keeps one cool in summer and warm in winter. I recommend that you wrap your tarot deck in silk, velvet, a special cloth, or a pouch. Or you may like to keep your tarot deck in a wooden box with appropriate crystals. The way you store your tarot deck is a personal decision, so look within to see what feels right. Change containers if the silk, pouch, or box you are using no longer holds the magic for you that it once had.

A Tarot Altar

AN ALTAR IS A PLACE for material objects that have a special significance for you and represent your inner self. The perfect place for your wrapped tarot deck is on an altar that you create. An altar can be made on a table top, dresser, or any surface. We unconsciously decorate surfaces and make altars and refer to them as interior design. For example, the dresser decorated with an arrangement of seashells gathered from a beach vacation represents the element water (cups). Or a collection of crystals artistically arranged is a form of an altar to the earth (pentacles/disks).

The tarot deck on your altar can be surrounded by symbols of the four elements. Fire is symbolized by candlesticks and candles. Water is symbolized by a vase or chalice. Air is symbolized by a fan, feathers, or an incense burner. Earth is symbolized by crystals, rocks, gemstones, or plants. Fresh or silk flowers, photographs, objects from nature, art such as sculpture or crafts, and things you have made are appropriate objects for an altar. Replace fresh flowers as soon as they begin to wilt. Do not use dried flowers or dry potpourri because they are devoid of energy and life force.

The Old, Loved, and Well-Used Tarot Deck

WHEN YOUR TAROT DECK IS OLD and falling apart to the point where you can no longer shuffle the cards, bury the deck under a tree. In this way, the deck returns to earth. Symbolically, the tree has roots that reach down to the earth and water, and branches that reach up to air and fire (sun). The tree encompasses the cyclic renewal of seed, sprout, bud, flower, fruit, and ripened fruit which falls to the ground to spread seed for new growth as the cycle continues.

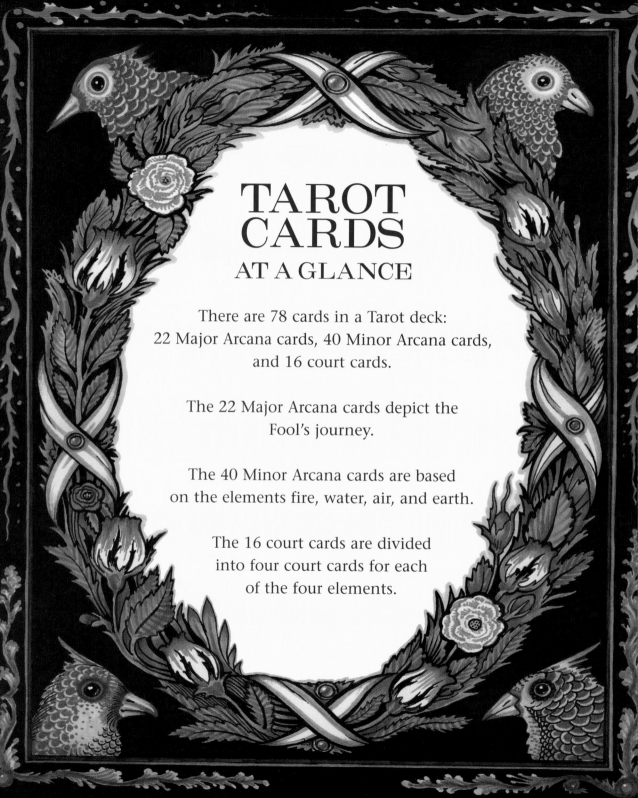

TAROT CARDS
AT A GLANCE

There are 78 cards in a Tarot deck:
22 Major Arcana cards, 40 Minor Arcana cards,
and 16 court cards.

The 22 Major Arcana cards depict the
Fool's journey.

The 40 Minor Arcana cards are based
on the elements fire, water, air, and earth.

The 16 court cards are divided
into four court cards for each
of the four elements.

THE MAJOR ARCANA

FOOL 0:	New opportunities
MAGICIAN 1/MAGUS 1:	Magical strength
PRIESTESS 2:	Receptivity, intuition
EMPRESS 3:	Harvest
EMPEROR 4:	Dominance
HIEROPHANT 5:	Structure
LOVERS 6:	Love and harmony
CHARIOT 7:	Clear path
STRENGTH 8 (RIDER-WAITE):	Strength and power
ADJUSTMENT 8 (CROWLEY THOTH):	Balance
HERMIT 9:	Inner quest
WHEEL OF FORTUNE 10:	Expansion, luck
JUSTICE 11 (RIDER-WAITE):	Truth
LUST 11 (CROWLEY THOTH):	Lust for life
HANGED MAN 12:	Stuck, surrender
DEATH 13:	Ending, transformation
TEMPERANCE 14/ART 14:	Artistic creativity
DEVIL 15:	Confusion, deceit
TOWER 16:	Radical change
STAR 17:	Self-realization, healing
MOON 18:	Evolution, gradual change
SUN 19:	Success, radiance
JUDGMENT 20/AEON 20:	Rebirth
WORLD 21/UNIVERSE 21:	Unlimited wonder

THE MINOR ARCANA

WANDS

ACE:	Do, action
TWO:	Set goals
THREE:	Virtuous actions
FOUR:	Completed projects
FIVE:	Strife
SIX:	Victory
SEVEN:	Valor yet struggle
EIGHT:	Swiftness
NINE:	Strength, holding your ground
TEN:	Oppression

SWORDS

ACE:	Think
TWO:	Peace of mind
THREE:	Sorrow due to loss
FOUR:	Truce and rest
FIVE:	Defeat
SIX:	Science, balance
SEVEN:	Futility, theft
EIGHT:	Interference, confusion
NINE:	Self-inflicted cruelty
TEN:	Ruin

CUPS

ACE:	Intuit, feel
TWO:	Love, partnership amongst equals
THREE:	Emotional abundance
FOUR:	(Rider-Waite) Rejection
FOUR:	(Crowley) Luxury, excess
FIVE:	Disappointment, depression
SIX:	Pleasure, joy
SEVEN:	Debauchery, chaos
EIGHT:	Indolence, laziness
NINE:	Happiness
TEN:	Satisfaction, contentment

PENTACLES/DISKS

ACE:	Manifestation, money
TWO:	Change
THREE:	Good work, hard work
FOUR:	(Rider-Waite) Greed
FOUR:	(Crowley) Power, foundation
FIVE:	Worry, poverty
SIX:	Success
SEVEN:	Delayed success, failure
EIGHT:	Prudence, pragmatism
NINE:	Gain
TEN:	Wealth

Who Are the Court Cards?

THE 16 COURT CARDS = 4 ELEMENTS X 4 PERSONALITIES

	FIRE	WATER	AIR	EARTH
Mature Feminine	Queen of Wands	Queen of Cups	Queen of Swords	Queen of Pentacles/Disks
Mature Masculine	King of Wands	King of Cups	King of Swords	King of Pentacles
In the Crowley deck, the mature masculine is the Knight.				
Child Feminine	Page/Princess of Wands	Page/Princess of Cups	Page/Princess of Swords	Page/Princess of Pentacles/Disks
Child Masculine	Knight of Wands	Knight of Cups	Knight of Swords	Knight of Pentacles
In the Crowley deck, the masculine child is the Prince.				

QUEEN OF WANDS: Express your creativity and power

KING OF WANDS: Strength, respect, and successful enterprise

KNIGHT OF WANDS: The path ahead is clear for dynamic action

PAGE OF WANDS: Good luck, opportunities, gain

PRINCE OF WANDS: Goals can be attained but it is best to act swiftly

PRINCESS OF WANDS: Lighten up, dance, and celebrate

QUEEN OF CUPS:	Emotional maturity, trust and follow your intuition
KING OF CUPS:	Kindness, charity, and artistic potential
KNIGHT OF CUPS:	Fortune, advancement, salvation
PAGE OF CUPS:	Good luck, fortunate news, opportunity
PRINCE OF CUPS:	Transformation, dive through levels of perception
PRINCESS OF CUPS:	Creative, simple, playful, a free spirit

QUEEN OF SWORDS:	Intelligence, keen perception; a person alone
KING OF SWORDS:	Focused and directed ideas; very mental
KNIGHT OF SWORDS:	Ideas, conflict, options; network and brainstorm
PAGE OF SWORDS:	Reaction, defense; methods are harsh and stormy
PRINCE OF SWORDS:	Clear, consistent, sharp, focused
PRINCESS OF SWORDS:	Allow strife, troubles, and worries to collapse

QUEEN OF PENTACLES/DISKS:	Prosperity, wealth, security, comfort
KING OF PENTACLES:	Money connected, solid as a rock, reliable, strong
KNIGHT OF PENTACLES/DISKS:	Stagnation, lull in activities, fallow fields
PAGE OF PENTACLES:	Prosperity, learning how the material world functions
PRINCE OF DISKS:	Solid and reliable in practical matters, order
PRINCESS OF DISKS:	Apprenticeship, new learning, practical craft or trade

GLOSSARY

AKASHIC RECORD: The summation of all creation in its past, present, and future forms.

ALCHEMY: The art and science of transforming base metal into gold.

ALEPH: Hebrew letter translated as "ox" and associated with the Fool card in the Thoth deck.

ALPHABET: A series of letters that are the basis of language. Derived from the first two letters of the Hebrew alphabet, which are aleph and beth.

AMRIT: Sanskrit word for sweet nectar, the ambrosial drink of enlightenment.

ANIMA: Latin for "soul." A Jungian psychological term that describes the feminine qualities in a man.

ANIMUS: Derived from the Latin word for "soul." A Jungian psychological term that describes the masculine qualities in a woman.

ASHRAM: Sanskrit word for a location where people live in spiritual community.

AYIN: Hebrew letter translated as "eye" and associated with the Devil card in the Thoth deck.

AYURVEDIC MEDICINE: Ancient healing system developed in East India. Ayurveda means "life" in Sanskrit, which is an ancient East Indian language.

BA-GUA: Chinese for "eight trigrams" used in feng shui and other Taoist arts. "Ba" means eight and "gua" means trigram.

BETH: Hebrew letter translated as "house" and associated with the Magus card in the Thoth deck.

BINAH: A mother goddess in the Hebrew tradition.

BINAH: A place of light on the Kabbalistic tree of life, symbolizing understanding, the womb, and the primal mother.

CADUCEUS: Wand made of two intertwined serpents used by the Roman god Mercury (Greek Hermes).

CHAKRA: "Wheel" in ancient East Indian language Sanskrit. Chakras are energy centers in the body.

CHESED: A place of light on the Kabbalistic tree of life, symbolizing loving kindness, mercy, and compassion.

CHETH: Hebrew letter translated as "fence" and associated with the Chariot card in the Thoth deck.

CHOKMAH: A place of light on the Kabbalistic tree of life symbolizing wisdom, paternal energy, and the father archetype.

DALETH: Hebrew letter translated as "door" and associated with the Empress card in the Thoth deck.

DORJES: Wands used in Tibetan Buddhist ritual to symbolize fire, thunder, and masculine energy.

DOSHAS: An elemental category of ancient East Indian medicine known as ayurveda.

FENG SHUI: The ancient Chinese art of placement. Pronounced "fung shway" and translated as wind and water.

GEBURAH: A place of light on the Kabbalistic tree of life symbolizing judgment, strength, and restraint.

GIMEL: Hebrew letter translated as "camel" and associated with the Priestess card in the Thoth deck.

HATHOR: An ancient Egyptian mother goddess usually depicted as a cow.

HEH: Hebrew letter translated as "window" and associated with the Star card in the Thoth deck.

HOD: A place of light on the Kabbalistic tree of life symbolizing splendor, glory, and submission to God.

IKIBANA: The Zen Japanese art of flower arrangement based on the relationship between heaven, humanity, and earth. Zen is the Japanese form of Buddhism.

JEHOVAH: A father god in the Hebrew tradition.

KABBALAH: The ancient Hebrew mystical tradition whereby one is united with both the masculine and feminine face of God.

KABBALISTIC TREE OF LIFE: A way of organizing spiritual energy symbolized by a tree with ten points of light, starting above with the highest light as it descends to earth.

KALPH: Hebrew letter translated as "palm of the hand" and associated with the Wheel of Fortune card in the Thoth deck.

KAPHA: The elements water and earth in the ancient East Indian language Sanskrit, used in ayurvedic medicine.

KARMA: Sanskrit for "action." A Buddhist concept of cause and effect, how kind actions create beneficial results.

KETHER: A place of light on the Kabbalistic tree of life symbolizing absolute unity and the number one.

KUNDALINI: Sanskrit term for the life force in our bodies that starts at the base of the spine and moves upward.

LAMED: Hebrew letter translated as "cattle prod" and associated with the Adjustment card in the Thoth deck.

MAJOR ARCANA: The "greater secret" that refers to the 22 tarot cards that begin with 0 The Fool and end with 21 The World/ Universe.

MALKUTH: A place of light on the Kabbalistic tree of life symbolizing the world of action and the material realm.

MANDALA: An artistic balanced geometric pattern to inspire meditation and spirituality.

MEM: Hebrew letter translated as "water" and associated with the Hanged Man card in the Thoth deck.

MINOR ARCANA: The "lesser secret" that refers to the 40 tarot cards numbered Ace through ten of the four suits wands, cups, swords, and pentacles/disks.

NETZACH: A place of light on the Kabbalistic tree of life symbolizing victory and dominance.

NUN: Hebrew letter translated as "fish" and associated with the Death card in the Thoth deck.

PEH: Hebrew letter translated as "mouth" and associated with the Tower card in the Thoth deck.

PENTACLE: A five-pointed star (pentagram) contained within a circle.

PITTA: The element fire in the ancient East Indian language Sanskrit, used in ayurvedic medicine.

QUERENT: The person receiving a tarot card reading.

QUOPH: Hebrew letter translated as the "back of the hand" and associated with the Moon card in the Thoth deck.

READER: The person doing a tarot card reading.

REINCARNATION: Buddhist belief that we have lived many lives prior to this one (also reincarnated).

RESH: Hebrew letter translated as "face" and associated with the Sun card in the Thoth deck.

RUNE STONES: A primitive northern European alphabet with symbolic meaning. The letters are often incised into stones.

SAMADI: Sanskrit term for a blissful enlightenment experience of unity of body, mind, and spirit.

SAMEKH: Hebrew letter translated as "prop" and associated with the Art card in the Thoth deck.

SAMSARA: In the Buddhist tradition, a Sanskrit word for the endless cycles of reincarnation that eventually led to enlightenment.

SEPHIROTH: A Hebrew term for the ten points of light on the Kabbalistic tree of life.

SHAMAN: Medicine man or woman in contact with spiritual realms for healing.

SHIN: Hebrew letter translated as "tooth" and associated with the Aeon card in the Thoth deck.

SHIVA: A deity of the ancient Vedic divine trinity of Brahma the creator, Vishnu the preserver, and Shiva the destroyer. The eye of Shiva is depicted on the Tower card in the Thoth deck.

TAROT: A collection of 78 picture cards comprised of 22 major trumps, 40 minor cards based on fire, water, air, and earth, and 16 royal figures.

TAV: Hebrew letter translated as "end" and associated with the Universe card in the Thoth deck.

TETH: Hebrew letter translated as "serpent" and associated with the Lust card in the Thoth deck.

THOTH: The ancient Egyptian god of communication, medicine, and metaphysical wisdom. He is depicted as a human with an ibis head or an ape head.

TIPHARETH: A place of light on the Kabbalistic tree of life symbolizing beauty, balance, and harmony.

TORA: The "Old Testament" books of Genesis, Exodus, Leviticus, Numbers, and Deuteronomy.

TOTEM: An animal spirit, the essence of a specific animal.

TOUJOURS L'AMOUR: French for "always love."

TZADDI: Hebrew letter translated as "fishhook" and associated with the Emperor card in the Thoth deck.

VATA: The element air or wind in the ancient East Indian language Sanskrit, used in ayurvedic medicine.

VAV: Hebrew letter translated as "nail" and associated with the Hierophant card in the Thoth deck.

YANG: A Chinese term for masculine energy. Yang qualities are hot, fast, dry, and active.

YESOD: A place of light on the Kabbalistic tree of life symbolizing foundation, ego, and sexuality.

YGGDRASIL: A sacred tree of Norse mythology.

YIN: A Chinese term for feminine energy. Yin qualities are cold, slow, wet, and receptive.

YOD: The first letter of the name of the Hebrew god Yehovah (Jehovah). It symbolizes fire and is associated with the Hermit card in the Thoth deck.

YOGA: Sanskrit word meaning union.

ZAIN: Hebrew letter translated as "sword" and associated with the Lovers card in the Thoth deck.

AUTHOR'S RECOMMENDATIONS

MUCH MORE CAN BE LEARNED ABOUT TAROT CARDS by viewing many different tarot decks. Order a tarot catalogue from U.S. Games Systems, Inc. and have some fun. Call 1-800-544-2637 or go to the web site www.usgamesinc.com. You'll find everything from the classic **RIDER-WAITE DECK** to **THE LORD OF THE RINGS TAROT.**

To discover the exact days of the new moons, full moons, equinoxes, and solstices to do tarot readings, I recommend the **WE'MOON ASTROLOGY CALENDAR.** We'Moon is published each year by Mother Tongue Ink. Call toll free 877-693-6666 or email wemoon@teleport.com if you do not find a We'Moon at your local metaphysical bookstore.

For those who want to know more about the **RIDER-WAITE DECK**, read *Seventy-Eight Degrees of Wisdom* by Rachel Pollack (Thorson's). This outstanding tarot classic contains in-depth essays on each of the seventy-eight cards. For those using the **CROWLEY THOTH DECK**, read his tarot classic *The Book of Thoth* (Samuel Weiser). In *The Book of Thoth,* Crowley uses the word "atu" to mean a Major Arcana card, and he refers to the I-Ching hexagrams as "Yi-King." An easy introduction to the I-Ching is included in my book *Taoist Feng Shui* (Destiny Books). A superb book on tarot is the companion book to **THE RENAISSANCE TAROT DECK** by Brian Williams. The author was a scholar of Italian Renaissance art and literature and brought his extensive knowledge to this information-packed book.

A thorough tarot workbook is *Tarot for YourSelf* by Mary K. Greer (Career Press, Inc.) who has written an outstanding series of tarot books. My favorite is *The Essence of Magic* (Career Press, Inc.) for practical esoteric information about tarot and aromatherapy. A modern book about the

CROWLEY THOTH DECK is *The Tarot Handbook* by Angeles Arrien (Putnam Publishing Group), which discusses psychological and cultural meanings of the cards.

Historical Importance

If the original tarot cards of the Renaissance are of interest to you, purchase the **VISCONTI-SFORZA PIERPONT MORGAN TAROCCHI DECK**. This deck is an accurate reproduction of the one commissioned by the Visconti-Sforza family in 15th century Milan. The original cards are divided between the Pierpont Morgan library in New York, the Accademia Carrara, and the Colleoni family of Bengamo, Italy. This is not a beginner's deck because the Minor Arcana depict arranged objects. (For example, the FOUR OF WANDS shows four balanced staves.) Though the deck is twice the cost of most other tarot decks, it has great historical value and brings the Renaissance to life. To continue in this line of study, next try the **CARY-YALE VISCONTI TAROCCHI** and Brian William's **MINCHIATE TAROT**. The original Visconti deck is in the Cary collection of playing cards at Yale University. The Minchiate includes cards not found in any other tarot deck such as cards for astrology signs. Other historical decks are the **GOLDEN DAWN TAROT DECK** and the French classic **TAROT OF MARSEILLES DECK**. Also of interest is the **RUSSIAN TAROT OF ST. PETERSBURG**, which is based on Russian folk tales and legends.

Feminist Tarots

Important modern feminist tarot decks are the **MOTHERPEACE TAROT DECK** by Vicki Noble and Karen Vogel, and the **DAUGHTERS OF THE MOON TAROT** by Ffiona Morgan. These decks are unique because they are round in shape and interpret tarot with a woman-identified feminist perspective. Another feminist deck is **THE SHINING TRIBE TAROT** (formerly **SHINING WOMAN**) by Rachel Pollack. Interestingly, in this deck the four Minor Arcana suits are renamed trees for fire, rivers for water, birds for air, and stones for earth. The **MEDICINE WOMAN TAROT DECK** by Carol Bridges also renames the Minor Arcana cards. Another matriarchal tarot deck is **THE BARBARA WALKER TAROT.** Her book, *The Woman's Encyclopedia of Myths and Secrets* (Harper San Francisco) is a classic of the women's spirituality movement. **THE GODDESS TAROT DECK** by Kris Waldherr is beautiful and includes Goddesses from many cultures.

Collage Imagery

For a tarot deck that is different than any other deck you've seen before, I recommend the **VOYAGER TAROT DECK** by James Wanless. The collage images are stunning. Another collage deck that uses some digital imagery is **THE COSMIC TRIBE TAROT** by Stevee Postman. Pagans will love this deck. It is strikingly different, yet classical tarot. **THE WILLIAM BLAKE TAROT** by Ed Buryn is made of delightful collages of the drawings and poetry of visionary artist William Blake. Most interesting is the author's renaming of the Minor Arcana.

Student Favorites

Some of my students use the **HANSON-ROBERTS TAROT DECK** by Mary Hanson-Roberts because of its magical fairy tale qualities. Some use the **CONNOLLY TAROT DECK** by Peter Paul Connolly because that deck, too, has a fairy tale feel. Another student favorite is the **TAROT OF THE SPIRIT DECK** by Pamela Eakins because of its beauty. Students also appreciate the wisdom of the **ANCESTRAL PATH**

TAROT DECK by Julia Cuccia-Watts. The **GREENWOOD TAROT DECK** by Mark Ryan and Chesca Potter is especially favored for its animal imagery. Fans of Arthurian lore enjoy the **ARTHURIAN TAROT** by Caitlin Matthews.

Cat Tarots

TAROT OF THE CAT PEOPLE DECK by Karen Kuykendall and the **GATTI ORIGINALI (FELINE)** are perfect for cat lovers, although the Gatti Originali contains only the Major Arcana. Occasionally, a student prefers to read with only the 22 Major Arcana cards. That's fine with me, but be prepared to see the DEATH card more often than it would usually appear if all 78 cards were used.

Herbs *and* Flowers

For those who love all things green, try the **HERBAL TAROT DECK** by Michael Tierra and Candis Cantin Packard, **THE FLOWER SPEAKS DECK** by Marlene Rudginsky, **THE TAROT OF HELLEN** by Valerie Bernard, and the **POWER OF FLOWERS DECK** by Isha Lerner. These decks can bring you much joy.

Artist's Tarots

The Spanish Surrealist artist Salvador Dali created a tarot deck called **DALI UNIVERSAL TAROT DECK**. This is an exceptional (and costly) collector's item of interest to both tarot readers and artists. Another artist's deck is the **ENCHANTED TAROT DECK** by Amy Zerner. These delicate and graceful cards depict photographs of large colorful tapestries.

Great Variety

The blossoming of tarot decks in the last century allows many decks to choose from. There are tarot decks for all interests. **THE LORD OF THE RINGS TAROT** by Terry Donaldson, Peter Pracownik, and Mike Fitzgerald is perfect for fans of the J.R.R. Tolkien books. **THE MYTHIC TAROT** by astrologer Liz Greene and Juliet Sharman-Burke draws inspiration from classical Greek myths and legends. **KABBALAH CARDS** by Ron Feldman and **TAROT OF THE SEPHIROTH** by Dan Staroff are inspired by the Kabbalah. **THE HALLOWEEN TAROT DECK** by Kipling West is lots of fun during Halloween season. A tarot deck that children can use is the **WHIMSICAL TAROT DECK** by Mary Hanson-Roberts. Not to be missed is the **WHEEL OF CHANGE** tarot by Alexandra Genetti.

There are many more wonderful tarot decks that I could recommend, but this should keep you busy for many birthdays to come.

Tarot *and the* Classics

To better understand myth and symbol, read *Memories, Dreams, Reflections* by Carl Jung (Vintage Books). Then read classic literature and great novels to understand tarot archetypes. Through characterization in novels, tarot archetypes come to life.

The one tarot card that my students and clients have the most problem understanding is the HANGED MAN. The novel *Things Fall Apart* (Doubleday & Company Inc.) by the Nigerian author Chinua Achebe, explains the many levels of the HANGED MAN. To understand the QUEEN OF SWORDS, read Pushkin's "The Queen of Spades," which is perhaps the best short story in world literature, in *Alexander Pushkin, Complete Prose*

Fiction (Stanford University Press). To comprehend the subtle nuances of the Minor Arcana CUPS suit, read *The Diaries of Anais Nin* (Harcourt).

Study the classics, seeking Major Arcana archetypes hidden in the pages. Could an aspect of the MAGICIAN lurk in Oscar Wilde's *The Picture of Dorian Gray* (Oxford University Press)? Is the TOWER the card for Mary Shelley's *Frankenstein* (Bantam, Doubleday, Dell Publishing Group)? If you actually sit down and read it, you will discover a classic of Romanticism more suited to the LOVERS than the TOWER of popular film. What is the card for Alighieri Dante's *Inferno* (Oxford University Press)? It is obvious which tarot archetype inspired Leo Tolstoy's short story "The Three Hermits."

Read collections of short stories too, such as *Best Short Stories* by Guy de Maupassant (Dover). Each of de Maupassant's stories correlates to a tarot card. Try to match each story with a card. The modern Italian author Italo Calvino did just that in *The Castle of Crossed Destinies* (Harcourt). He illustrated his book with two Medieval European tarot decks to create short stories.

Stick with the classics. Find the hidden tarot archetypes as you read.

ABOUT THE AUTHOR

Susan Levitt is a professional tarot card reader, astrologer, and feng shui consultant in the San Francisco Bay Area. She is the author of *Teen Feng Shui, Taoist Feng Shui,* and *Taoist Astrology.* Susan maintains a website at www.susanlevitt.com.

TAROT CARD SOURCE LIST

Illustrations in this book include artwork from several other tarot decks. The list provided here identifies the deck from which the artwork was taken, and the page number(s) where the illustrations appear in this book.:

Connolly Tarot: pgs. 8, 98, 113, 136, 216

Faerie Tarot: pg. 74

Hanson Roberts Tarot: pg. 25

New Palladini Tarot: pg. 230

Old English Tarot: pgs. 26, 35, 53, 80, 118, 156, 180, 181, 200

Oswald Wirth Tarot: pg. 16

Power of Flowers: 169, 170, 221

Rennaissance Tarot: pg. 183

SPECIAL ILLUSTRATION NOTE: The Feng Shui tortoise on pages 188 and 190–193 is from an original painting by Brian Williams, and appears courtesy of the author.